For S.F.D.

Other works from Serpent Club Press:

2013
Moon on Water
Matthew Gasda

2014
Autumn, Again; Spring, Anew
Michael Skelton and Stephen Morel

On Bicycling: An Introduction
Samuel Atticus Steffen

2015
Sonata for Piano and Violin
Matthew Gasda

(Forthcoming in 2015)
Circumambulate
Daniel Bossert

The Substitute
Michael Skelton

New Writing
Volume I

A Compilation

Serpent Club Press

NEW WRITING: VOLUME I
Copyright © Serpent Club Press, 2015
All rights reserved

Serpent Club Press books may be purchased for educational, business, or sales
promotional use. For more information please contact Serpent Club Press at
theserpentclub@gmail.com

First Edition

Printed in the United States of America
Set in Williams Caslon
Designed by Emily Gasda

ISBN
9780990664338

LCCN
2015943484

PREFACE

"But when the mind opens, and reveals the laws which traverse the universe, and make things what they are, then shrinks the great world at once into a mere illustration and fable of this mind. What am I? and What is? asks the human spirit with a curiosity new-kindled, but never to be quenched. Behold these outrunning laws, which our imperfect apprehension can see tend this way and that, but not come full circle. Behold these infinite relations, so like, so unlike; many, yet one. I would study, I would know, I would admire forever. These works of thought have been the entertainments of the human spirit in all ages."

– Ralph Waldo Emerson

The function of American culture seems to be to prevent the act of solitary reading and writing. This does not seem debatable, to me, because the terms of the debate have been rendered incomprehensible by the merging of consciousness with the flow of information on the internet; by our insistence on extending our consciousness through electronic devices at every point along the continuum of waking life. The question of creating literature—of being a literary artist—is now defined in relation to technology: the question of what literature can be in 2015 is conditioned by the more fundamental question of whether literature can 'be' anything other than a less-than-singular manifestation of digital content-production.

I do not write this from a place of indifference: my own life, my own attempt to be a writer—to mediate my life through literature (a word which implies a tradition)—is fully conditioned by this technological context. If concentration—on the word, on *logos*—is a method of prayer, than it is a method whose intricate steps are being forgotten or confused. The symbolic process of self-overhearing—of listening to oneself as one thinks—has become subordinate to representing oneself through the internet (the image). No longer readers, we are *transfixers*, who would fuse ourselves, permanently, with a composite self-image—free from the wearisome business of creative self-evolution. As 'transfixers' we reject reading, because reading means swimming under the surface of the composite image; it means swimming under the surface of information.

Content cannot be poetry and we prefer it that way: content is inert, it does not speak back into us and through us the way literature does. Literature, and more generally, art, has always been an unwanted byproduct of modernity. Modern culture wants self-consciousness without the self: talk of the self by people who are not capable of cultivating one. This is the essence of post-internet culture: selfhood without a self; selfhood without the difficult work of soul-making.

Even the term 'post-internet' seems anachronistic. We seem now, in 2015, to be in a post-app, post-phone culture: a culture defined by the search for material efficiency in all domains of human activity. Literature (taken as a name for a kind of writing and reading) cannot survive in an efficiency culture: it is driven beyond the gates of culture, it is made a refugee.

And this does not mean that the book is dead: the book lives on, physically and digitally, as do commercial presses. What has died are the guiding spirits that animate the task of writing, printing, and disseminating books. Books, on the whole, no longer constitute 'literature'; making literature not only a refugee, but a ghost.

Is this a statement of despair? Not entirely—it is an attempt at approximation, at rendering what it feels like to love and believe in the aesthetic and existential possibilities of the written word in a time when those possibilities are being foreclosed upon.

2

Literature, whether directly or indirectly, is about suffering. Suffering and literature were born together in Greek tragedy. Literature begins with the question: would it be better not to have been born at all, than to suffer in this way?

I would not say that the pieces in this volume are tragic or particularly filled with suffering, but I want to suggest that suffering is in the foreground of all these pieces: as the motivation for writing in the first place.

3

Literature is the writing that we adore, elevate, desire—that we believe in— without knowing fully why.

4

Literature is an ecosystem of values: it has its ferns, its flowers, its bushes, its saplings, its ancient trees. It is an organism as adaptable as a forest: it survives fires, logging, pollution; it survives despite us and our critical interventions. We shouldn't 'map' literature, or literary texts: we should walk through them, sample them; we should adapt ourselves to the textual environment: because there is no defining literature, there is only embedding ourselves within it.

5

This anthology of new writers and writing is not meant to be in any way representative of an era, of a *geist*, of a style. For the most part, the following writers are my friends. This anthology is therefore an act of love and encouragement: it is meant to represent the conversations, ideas, and tropes that defined certain relationships and moments.

It is, however, also an act of self-criticism: it is meant to show, to tease out, to reveal the patterns present in a cross-section of a certain community tissue sample.

It is meant to show how a community of writers mirrors a universe of writers; how a community of texts mirrors a universe of texts.

6

In short: this anthology is part of an organic process. It is a garden for refugees and ghosts.

A seedling.

Matthew Gasda
Editor, Serpent Club Press

Contents

December 17th
Eda

We are in love all over again, and I know, watching his face from the train as he stands on the platform, that I love him so dearly, so inextricably, that our two lives are one in a way that they were not before this moment.

And when I look at him as he walks toward me then there is nothing else (and it's a singular happiness, connected to him, because of him, and it is the fullest happiness, and it is so full of potential).

SWEDEN
Eda

I still feel apart from this, and haven't had the meditative time, haven't had the wandering time I need: we always have a map and a goal and there's so little surprise. But I hear wolves cry in the distance! (And that's something I've never heard before). It's a melancholy but very high pitched noise: not the long, deep howl I imagined as a child growing up, having never heard one before.

HONESTY
Eda

It seems to me that my chronic discontentment arises out of a general dishonesty about what I want. Nothing comes into shape as I'd like it to, because I never vocalize my imagination or act it out (though I think vocalization is more important at least for now, since it often promotes and pre-empts action).

Vacation in Sweden feels too much like being at home, but I never described to O— my dreams of being completely away from people, near a lake, in the sun all day, bathing and washing in the water, living so differently from life in the city, so that the day goes slowly by.

I wanted to return a different person: my dreams always imagine me as a better version of myself, and I never told him about this, never told anyone.

I often feel I make so little progress in any number of things. My life has been so much a fantasy occurring entirely in my mind, and the simplest things are not expressed.

(Different, more confusing things are expressed, but rarely as simple truths).

I wonder if I seem a dishonest person? (My mother says I make people uncomfortable and thinks that it's largely due to my unclear intentions).

Oh, all the people I've let slip away from me, or that I failed to catch for even a short time.

I should become more versed in quickly capturing people.

The Other Side of Utility: Lolita, Improvisation, and the Moral Use of the Novel
Tony Ferrizzi

This began as a paper about *Lolita* and the moral utility of literature. And I will say something about that—I promise I will—but first I need to say something else. What I will say—eventually—is that *Lolita* is an ethically useful novel because it is an example of literary improvisation. But I am using the word "improvisation" in an idiosyncratic way, and so I ought to say something about improvisation before I say something about how Lolita improvises and why that matters to ethical utilty.

Improvisation is more than extemporizing and it is not the same thing as spontaneous composition. It is not the opposite of forethought but of determinacy, whether spontaneous or not. Improvisation is call and response, attention and reaction—what Bergson calls "intuition" and what Deleuze calls "counter-actualization."

Improvisation is attending to and entering into that which is, as Bergson says, "unique and consequently inexpressible." It is a matter of making contact with the singularity of an object or event. Getting beneath representation, breaking through representation, no longer seeing the object as an instance of some type—no longer seeing it conceptually—but touching it, rubbing right up against it and into it, and feeling it in its uniqueness. Intuiting it. Entering into it rather than going around it.

The improviser begins by intuiting. She hears the call, feels it, rides it and enters into it. But she also has to respond to it. And here is Deleuze: you have to counter-actualize. Counter-actualization is taking what happens to you, using its power, and filling it up with your own material. It is peeling the event away from its original context and retaining only its "splendor." Impregnating the event so that what is born belongs equally to you and to it.

Deleuze and I have a topological disagreement. I want responding to an event to be a way of entering into that event, into its uniqueness, to plunge down into the depths of the world rather than spinning off on the surface (as Deleuze has it). But that topological matter is not important here. What's important is that for both Deleuze and me counter-actualization is an act of freedom—maybe the only act of freedom in a world that determines us—and that the new, resulting event does not belong to your subject but to the event that is impregnated by that freedom and to you, as a free actor, desubjectified, immersed in that event.

Improvisation is foundationally not an artistic but an ethical activity. Deleuze says of counter-actualization what I want to say of improvisation—that it is a matter of being worthy. He writes: "either ethics makes no sense at all, or this is what it means and has nothing else to say: not to be unworthy of what happens to us." To be worthy of what happens is to amor-fati-love-your-fate, to ask nothing to be other than what it is, but at the same time to become free, to break through representation in order to ride the power and singularity of what happens to you. To respond. To improvise.

I'm going to say that *Lolita*, as a novel, improvises, and that for that reason it is ethically useful. And to get there, I'm going to have to take seriously Nabokov's claim that *Lolita* is not fundamentally about the erotic love between Humbert Humbert and Dolores Haze. Here is Nabokov, gorgeously, in the 1957 essay "On a Book Entitled Lolita," which accompanied the 1958 publication of the novel:

> *There are gentle souls who would pronounce Lolita meaningless because it does not teach them anything. I am neither a reader nor a writer of didactic fiction, and [...] Lolita has no moral in*

tow. For me, a work of fiction exists only insofar as it affords me what I shall bluntly call aesthetic bliss, that is a sense of being somehow, somewhere connected with other states of being where art (curiosity, tenderness, kindness, ecstasy) is the norm.

[...] I have not reread Lolita since I went through the proofs in the spring of 1955 but I find it to be a delightful presence now that it quietly hangs about the house like a summer day which one knows to be bright behind the haze. And when I thus think of Lolita, I seem always to pick out for special delectation such images as Mr. Taxovich, or that class list of Ransdale School, or Charlotte saying "waterproof," or Lolita in slow motion advancing toward Humbert's gifts, or the pictures decorating the stylized garret of Gaston Godin, or the Kasbeam barber (who cost me a month of work), or Lolita playing tennis, or the hospital at Elphinstone, or pale, pregnant, beloved, irretrievable Dolly Schiller dying in Gray Star (the capital town of the book), or the tinkling sounds of the valley town coming up the mountain trail [...]. These are the nerves of the novel. These are the secret points, the subliminal co-ordinates by means of which the book is plotted—although I realize very clearly that these and other scenes will be skimmed over

or not noticed, or never even reached, by those
who begin reading the book under the impression
that it is something on the lines of Memoirs of a
Woman of Pleasure [...]

(Nabokov, 1957, pp. 314-316.)

The scenes that Nabokov selects for delectation, the nerves of *Lolita* are not scenes of passion. They are not extraordinary moments. They are rote, banal occasions—a class list, the pronunciation of a word, decorative pictures, a tennis match. They seem to be wholly accidental features of the novel. But if Nabokov is right—and I think that he is—these are where the magic is. And if he is right—and I think that he is—then what *Lolita* does is not draw us into erotic love, or obsession, or madness, but the glory of everyday events. The power of singularity.

Here's what I want to say: *Lolita* is an act of literary improvisation. Nabokov seems to want the novel to avoid ethics in every sense, but we know better than that—Humbert's affair with Dolores Haze just is ethically viable. On my reading, *Lolita* responds to that moral normativity that burdens it by intuiting morally problematic love, entering into Humbert's neuroses, and responding to and using the power of moral events. The erotic contact between Humbert Humbert and Dolores Haze, descriptions of which are conspicuously absent from the novel, fuel, from behind the curtain, the rich singularity of the banal occasions that for Nabokov were the nerves of Lolita. The novel counter-actualizes moral events, peeling them away, filling them with everyday banality, and uses their power to draw on that which is in everyday occasions unique and consequently inexpressible.

Let's take a look at one of *Lolita's* nerves—Lolita playing tennis. Here it is, in selections:

No hereafter is acceptable if it does not produce her as she was then, in that Colorado resort between Snow and Elphinstone, with everything right: the white wide little-boy shorts, the slender waist, the apricot midriff, the white breast-kerchief whose ribbons went up and encircled her neck to end behind in a dangling knot leaving bare her gaspingly young and adorable apricot shoulder blades with that pubescence and those lovely gentle bones, and the smooth, downward-tapering back. Her cap had a white peak. Her racket had cost me a small fortune.

[…] The exquisite clarity of all her movements had its auditory counterpart in the pure ringing sound of her every stroke. The ball when it entered her aura of control became somehow whiter, its

resilience somehow richer, and the instrument of precision she used upon it seemed inordinately prehensile and deliberate at the moment of clinging contact. Her form was, indeed, an absolutely perfect imitation of absolutely top-notch tennis—without any utilitarian results.

[…] My Lolita had a way of raising her bent left knee at the ample and springy start of the service cycle when there would develop and hang in the sun for a second a vital web of balance between toes, foot, pristine armpit, burnished arm and far back-flung racket, as she smiled up with gleaming teeth at the small globe suspended so high in the zenith of the powerful and graceful cosmos she had created for the express purpose of falling upon it with a clean resounding crack of her golden whip.

(Nabokov, 1955, pp.230-232.)

This scene is not about the erotic love between Humbert Humbert and Dolores Haze. It is not about erotic love at all. It is about the singularity of a banal occasion—the everyday uniqueness of Lolita's tennis game. It is about a kerchief, the sound of a tennis stroke, a raised left knee, an armpit—objects and events, glorious for their uniqueness, ordinarily unfelt, unattended to, encumbered by their banality.

Humbert is not immersed in Lolita's body as a sexual object. He is immersed in the unique power of her body in motion. He is lovingly and joyfully attending to the glory of that which would otherwise seem rote. What this scene does, what Lolita does, more than anything else, is draw us into the aesthetic joy of everyday events and their unique powers.

Lolita intuits banality, but it cannot avoid doing so from the side of moral power. This gives it a mechanism to respond to morality and to express everyday singularity. This is the mechanism by which it improvises, by which it is worthy of moral normativity, by which it responds to the call of the moral hegemony that weighs on it.

By improvising on the theme of moral power, and by using that power to express banal singularity, *Lolita* breaks through moral representation. Moral events are no longer in question as moral events, they are beyond the scope of moral hegemony. We are asked to move beyond morality and into aesthetics. By moving through moral representation, *Lolita* instates a new ethics—in which what this novel can do, what all novels can do, is improvise. Be worthy.

Pushing through morality is for *Lolita* a way of being worthy of that morality, by re-routing its power, by pushing itself into aesthetic enjoyment. What good is *Lolita*? It pushes through, it makes itself worthy, and in so doing it gives its author and its readers a chance to slip through the crack it has made. And so there is a Nabokovian utility of the novel: the other side of moral representation, the other side of utility.

POSTSCRIPT

This paper was meant to be about moral utility. I have said something about the way that *Lolita* pushes through utility, the way that it crosses over to the other side, but I haven't said very much about how that activity counts as a kind of utility itself. I want to say something about that now; and that means I have to say something about what that kind of breaking through does.

Lolita is useful because it counter-actualizes morality. Because it uses morality to push through moral hegemony, arriving finally at the joy of aesthetic interaction. And that kind of breaking through, that kind of aesthetic joy, which can only be arrived at by way of a counter-actualization, enacts what I want to say is one kind of justice.

Ordinarily, justice is the kind of thing you need to run a community. It is the business of moral philosophers and political theorists—part of a conversation inaugurated by *The Republic*, a conversation that is fundamentally about how to make prescriptions regarding people's behavior in communities. It is a matter of practical necessity—people live in communities, and so we better know how to act in those communities.

That kind of justice—ordinary justice—is important. But there is another kind of justice. This kind is both rare and ubiquitous—rare for its being not often the subject of conversation, and ubiquitous for its being the ever-present ground on which the first kind of justice lies. This is not ordinary justice; it is not a matter of making prescriptions for communal behavior. This is something deeper than that; it is the kind of justice that sits at the bottom of your being, weighing you down, keeping you plumb. Like a brass bob. It is the kind of justice that you would still have to worry about if you were alone on an island. Rather than answering the question "How should the members of our community behave?" it answers the question "How should I live my life?"

The first kind of justice is rightfulness. It begs the question "What is right?" and sets out to codify good behavior and bad behavior in terms of some kind of communal normativity. But the second kind of justice is righteousness: "How ought I live?" It is a matter of getting right, not with a community and its norms, but with you and whatever power you are a part of in the deepest possible sense, at the bottom of your existence.

What I want to say is that this second kind of desert island justice is what literature can speak to. Rightfulness is the way of lawmakers. But righteousness is the way of artists. If you want to get a law passed, there are lots of things you can do: writing a novel is not one of them. But if you want to feel the weight and power of a particular way of living your life, if you want to follow the line down to the plumb bob, then no number of letters to your congressman will do.

What *Lolita* encourages is a particularly strong form of desert island justice. It demands its audience to consider life according to rightfulness, but then by way of a sleight of hand it peels away, diving down, pushing through that rightfulness by way of its own power, arriving finally at a life lived righteously. That maneuver is prescriptive—it orders us to follow, to arrive ourselves at aesthetic joy. And by prescribing joy, *Lolita* prescribes a life of justice. After all, it is a good life.

No Answer
Sam Steffen

The man called Bark had just finished leaving a fourth message for his Wednesday afternoon appointment, who was by his count now thirty minutes late and therefore beyond the point of obliging his patience further, when he gave up waiting at the cafe, crossed Main Street, entered the Rugged-Star Hotel, ordered himself a gin and tonic with no ice at the bar and stationed himself at a small empty table near the lobby window. The hotel had large French windows which the man had been eyeing for quite some time from the café across the street, where his appointment had failed to show.

"Would you like a menu, sir?"

A woman dressed in a white uniform had appeared, and was suddenly standing beside him.

"What?" the man said, distractedly. "Ah, no. No, thank you." He raised his glass and made a motion as if to rattle the ice cubes, of which he had already forgotten he had requested none, and sloshed his drink upon his wrist in the fumbled indication that he was content.

"Waiting for someone?" she asked.

He laughed. Something about it struck him as very funny, but it was too complicated to explain just at the moment. "No," he said. "Not really. I'm alright." The woman nodded and left him. Wiping his arm with his cloth napkin, he returned his gaze to the small café across the street, where he had been sitting not more than three minutes before, and where he now anticipated, perhaps, encountering with his gaze—from a new remove—the man for whom he had indeed been waiting the past half-hour.

It was a warm spring day. The winter had been a long one and in the street was still the evidence of the melting season, slowly diminishing piles of snow and ice that had formed around and between parked vehicles. All the streets of Capernaum were wet with the thaw, a clean, fresh smell lay buoyant on the breeze, and the sun, which for the first time in months felt warm upon the skin, had apparently drawn the people out in droves. Who knew there were so many of them? The man they called Bark had become so accustomed to seeing on the street nobody but uniformed delivery-men and elderly people with small dogs that in recent months he was given to imagining that they were the only kind of person who lived in Capernaum—that the apartments over the restaurants on Main Street, and the clustered row-homes down along the riverfront and the statelier residential properties high upon the mountain—all of them were merely the lodging places of none other than delivery-men and the small-dogged-elderly. What other kind of person was there?

Of course, it was no great secret that this pigeonholed reasoning of his was merely a consequence of the winter, which to Bark's mind had a way of shrinking the imagination, just as it seemed to truncate the length of the days, the duration of gladness which occasionally followed meals, as well as one's feelings of hope about one's condition in life, generally speaking. As he sipped his drink and stared from the hotel lobby window out at the street, he tried to drink in all of the unexpected society he observed: the man across the street playing the guitar on a bench; a young couple immediately outside the window-sill, skipping; a bearded fellow in the street, between angularly-parked vehicles, lighting a cigarette; a young woman in a billowing coat pushing a stroller along with one hand and holding the hand of a little boy with the other; a man with a newspaper, disappearing into a chocolate-shop; a woman emerging from a hairdresser's across the way. It was a lovely day, and from where he sat at his empty table behind the french windows with his gin and tonic, it was like a private viewing of a spontaneous parade. Yes; it was the indescribable feeling of spring—the sort of day a man could spend in waiting indefinitely, without minding too much what for.

"Waiting for someone?" a woman's voice asked.

The man called Bark turned his eyes from the

scene outside and caught the face of a young woman seated at the table immediately opposite him. She was maybe thirty years old, thin, with elegant features and remarkable freckles spotting her nose and cheeks. If he had been concerned with anything other than obtaining a spot near the window across from the café where he had been waiting, he might have minded himself more in selecting his seat; as it was, the absence of company—his, hers—made their situation awkward, as though they had already been seated at opposite ends of the same long table, rather than opposing ends of two short ones.

He smiled, but did not laugh. "As a matter of fact, I am," he said. He pointed at the café with his drink in hand, and made like he was about to explain. "Well...actually, it's kind of a long story," he said.

She rose from her seat, shouldering her handbag as she did so, as though she meant to leave. Instead, she came nearer. "That's alright," she said, putting out her hand. He took it and shook it, expecting to get a name, but the woman only introduced herself by saying: "I'm waiting for someone, too. Do you mind?" She sat down at his table timidly without waiting for him to reply.

"By all means," he said. He seemed pleased with himself, suddenly, as though he had done something kind for which some congratulation was in order.

"Would you like a menu?" The waitress had materialized again, suddenly, holding two menus.

The man called Bark shook his head and raised his glass again, and was for the second time regretful that he had not ordered ice. The woman shook her head and the waitress left.

"So who are you waiting for?" the young woman said.

"I might ask you the same question." He was afraid to turn his eyes from the window, for fear that his appointment would show.

"Okay. I'll go first. I'm waiting for my husband," the young woman said. "It's terribly awkward, I'm afraid, but you see—well, he's in the army...or was in the army, I should say. Or was in the service. I guess he's still in the army—but he's back now. He was overseas until yesterday. Yesterday he got back and I'm waiting for him to get here. He's coming in from Fort Somethingerother—I can never remember the names of all the forts and bases—the one up in New York. Do you know the one I mean?"

The man called Bark shook his head and sipped his drink and flicked his eyes out the window across the street to the café where he had told his appointment to meet him.

"It's alright if you don't. I can't keep any of them straight. I guess I'm just a little nervous," the woman continued. "I haven't seen him in more than a year.

Do you know what that's like? To be married to someone you haven't seen in so long?"

A moment passed where he felt that she might actually be expecting an answer. Before he could say anything, she started up again.

"I'm sorry. I don't mean to be dumping on you like this. I don't even know you. It's just that I'm terribly *nervous*. God, look at me! I'm shaking. Isn't that funny? About meeting my own husband? You'd think I were about to go into a job interview or something."

"Seems natural to me," said Bark, sipping his drink, smugly. "Care for a drink?" he asked, thinking it might calm her down. From the way she was talking, it struck him that perhaps she had already had a few—several, maybe.

"I don't usually act this way with strangers," she said. "It's just that—well..." She sighed. "I'm sorry. I haven't let you talk at all. What did you say your name was?"

"Doug," the one they called Bark said, putting out his hand. He had forgotten until that moment that they had already shaken hands. She took his hand, but once more did not give up her name. "Pleasure."

"What was the story you were going to tell me?"

"Oh, it's nothing. Sort of needlessly complex. I wouldn't want to bore you."

"No," she said. "Please. I want to hear it. I'm all ears."

Bark sipped his drink. Outside there was no one even slightly resembling his 2:30. His eyes were fixed on the door of the café he had just come out of, from which a couple was now emerging, the man of whom he could see was picking his teeth with a toothpick, probably expressing satisfaction with his life and all its circumstances.

"Well," he said. He seemed to be weighing the matter in his own mind, considering whether it was worth all of the trouble of going into.

"Is it someone you're watching for out there?"

"Well—" Bark repeated. He sighed heavily and began with reluctance: "Do you see that café across the street there?" He pointed.

The woman looked. "Yes. Angelo's?"

"Yes. You see, well—I had an appointment with a man in there at 2:30 that was very important. It was more important for him than it was for me, you understand, and I was there at 2:30, precisely when we had agreed to meet, and he did not show up. I gave him every opportunity. I called his cellphone after ten minutes of waiting, then again after twenty. Then I got hungry and decided to go ahead and order. When the food was brought I tried him again. Then once more when I had finished. We had planned on having lunch together and there I was, having already finished lunch, feeling ready for a nap when I decided I would hop over here for a quick drink."

He paused, as if he doubted whether to tell her the next part—but because of how expectantly she seemed to be listening, he decided to simply go on.

"You see, I had a strange thought while I was in there waiting for my appointment. There I was at the window seat inside Angelo's, looking out at the street. Do you see the one I mean? You can see there's a group of young women being seated there now?"

The woman looked. "Yes," she said, squinting. Her gaze penetrated her own reflection as well as the front-glass of the café across the street, which reflected the goings-on of the bright spring day, behind which there were the impossibly silent figures the man described. "Yes, I think I do."

"Not five minutes ago I was over there," he said, "and I kept looking over here at the windows of this hotel, and I kept wondering to myself what it would be like to be here instead of there, and whether I might not just as easily wait for my appointment here as there. It seemed to me that in the café it was all I could do to wait for him. But *here*, you see—here I could be doing *anything*." After saying this he nearly did not go on. He felt suddenly as though he could not make himself understood, as though he had begun to explain something he could not finish and would rather not try. But perhaps because the day was so warm, he said, as if in very spite of this feeling: "The more I thought of it, the more attractive the idea became. So I paid for my lunch and hopped over here and here I am now."

The woman looked at him, expectantly. He did not go on. "I don't understand," she said.

The man called Bark looked at the woman. "Don't understand what?" he said, hoping to clarify.

"Who were you meeting?"

"Oh, just a client of mine."

"A client? What sort of work do you do?" He was about to tell her that he worked as a financial consultant for Briggman and Floss, but before he could answer the woman brightened suddenly and suggested with a smile: "Wait. Don't tell me. I bet I know. Are you some sort of *spy*?"

The sunlight outside the hotel seemed alarmingly bright. It was as though a small cluster of clouds that had been casting a faint shadow had dissolved in an instant and there was nothing to distinguish the moment from a midsummer's day. The man felt that he could actually see the snow-piles in the street shriveling up into nothing. Something about it emboldened him, made him eager for some sort of adventure. He felt as though anything had suddenly become possible. His imagination swelled: he could have been the president of a foreign stock exchange, he thought with exclamation. For a moment he felt that part of him—a sadder, humbler, truer part—was still waiting for the appointment in the café across the street, looking at him desperately from behind the glass, longing to know what life was like on the other side of the French windows.

"As a matter of fact," he said, cautiously, "I am. You've guessed it! Not a spy, exactly—but, you know. Private investigator is what we're called in the business."

"Oh boy!" the woman gushed. "How interesting!"

"It is," he said stupidly. "It really is."

"And you're meeting someone who hired you?" she guessed.

"Yes," he said. "That's right. I am."

"What was the job?"

"Oh..." he said, "Um, well..."

"Or are you not at liberty to discuss it?"

"Well, no—it's nothing like that. I mean, certain members of my profession would certainly frown upon it if they knew I was going to be dispensing with the details here and there, as it's all done strictly in confidence, you understand, but...you know— my feeling on the matter is that...well, my feeling is that so long as the parties involved have nothing to do with the recipients of the information, then what's the harm in it?"

He was surprised by his own mouth—that he had such things to say about a profession he knew almost nothing about. His heart had begun to race in his breast, and he felt certain that he could tell her anything now and she would believe him. His mind was alive with ideas. She looked out the window, across the street, towards the café.

"I can't name names, of course, but I what I can tell you is that it's one of those horrible jealousy cases you're always hearing about. The husband— he's the man I'm waiting for—hired me to do a little snooping on his wife and a few of her acquaintances. Of course, I've done my part. The results, I'm afraid, will only confirm what he already suspects and will probably result in…well, you know."

"Murder?" she asked, horrified.

The man they called Bark guffawed. "Murder?— Well! I should certainly hope not! But then again," he said, thinking twice about it, "now that you mention it, it *has* been known to go that way."

"That's a shame," the woman said.

"It is. It really is."

The woman looked out the window. Her mind seemed to be drifting away. High above them the clouds were gathering once more, and the street became overcast.

"But it's very rare," he said. "I was thinking more along the lines of divorce."

"Divorce?" she said with equal horror.

"Yes. It's really quite sad, actually, when you think about it."

"It's *terrible*," she said.

"Yes," he confirmed.

Something about the word seemed to have struck a chord with her. For a moment Bark watched her to see what would happen next. He sipped his drink. The woman seemed to be trying to decide something in her mind. He let her alone a moment and looked out the window where he saw, stopped at the traffic-light, a man sitting in the cab of a large pick-up truck. Something about the man seemed familiar, though he couldn't say he had ever seen him before. He had impeccably brushed hair and looked as if he had been cut from bronze.

"Say," the woman said, as though emerging from a trance. "I've been thinking something."

"What's that?" the one they called Bark said.

"I was wondering if I could ask a favor of you."

Bark's eyebrows raised. "A favor?"

"Well, I realize it's a bit forward of me—we've only just met. But I must tell you, Mr.—ah, Mr.—I mean, Doug...you seem like a man who's seen a lot of the world, who knows a thing or two about people."

"Yes," Bark agreed. He rather liked the way that sounded. "I suppose you could say that."

"I was wondering...if it's not too much trouble—Jesus! Look at me—I'm quivering all over!"

"It's alright," Bark said, gently. "You can ask, at least. There's no harm in asking."

"Well, it's just that...my husband. I was wondering if I could maybe introduce you to him when he arrives?"

He nearly choked at the question. He coughed once, and then said with alarm: "Introduce me? But...I mean...but why? I mean, I suppose there wouldn't be any harm in it. But—tell me why."

"I'm afraid that's the whole trouble," she said. "You see, my husband has been away a very long time. He's been away more than a year now, and he's coming home today. It's funny that we have to meet here at a hotel like this, but we—or I should say I—I live down in North Carolina. He's stationed in New York. We're meeting at this hotel because it's a halfway point for us. We'll spend the weekend in town here and then it'll be back to business as usual: I'll go back south, he'll go North, and who knows when our paths will meet again?"

Even though he knew instinctively that she was referring to her husband, the man they called Bark allowed himself for a moment to believe that she was talking about him.

"The thing about my husband is that he's a very worried man," she continued. "He worries about me a lot. He's always calling me up—even when he's in the most remote places—calling me up to tell me to make sure I go out with the girls and to remember to socialize a little, to get out more. I think he thinks I'm dependent on him or something…I don't know. It's just that that kind of living—going out with the ladies and socializing…it's just not for me. That's not really who I am. He doesn't know I guess because he's not really around enough to know. I don't blame him. It's his duties that keep him away. We've all got our duties, haven't we?"

Bark supposed we did.

"Anyhow, I was just wondering if I could introduce you—as…well, as a friend of mine, when he gets here. Just to set his mind at ease."

"You mean lie?" he said.

"Oh. Well, yes, I suppose. If you want to call it that. But it's really not so severe a thing as all that. It's just to set his mind at ease. Would you mind? And anyway, you seem like a good friend. I don't even suppose it would be a lie, would it? You could just meet him and then say you had to leave off right away—to meet your client. I just think it would do him so well to see me with…a friend. He just worries about me so much."

"I don't know," Bark said. The proposal and its explanation flustered him. He found the woman's request peculiar—so peculiar, in fact, that he could not be sure the woman did not have an ulterior motive in asking it. What was she trying to pull here? His mind raced.

"Please—" she urged. "It would mean a lot."

For a moment he wished he actually were a private investigator, that he really was waiting for a jealous husband to come and be ruined by his incriminating photographs and stories. If he were, he might know what to say. He tried to think of something.

"Oh, dear—what's wrong?" the woman said. "I've upset you haven't I?"

"No—It's not that—" Bark said. He began to feel like things were out of his hands now, that whoever this woman's husband was, he would be fast approaching, was maybe already on top of them, watching them scheme against him, gathering evidence with which to enact some sort of vengeance. Perhaps they were both being watched by someone—a real private investigator maybe? Perhaps she was staging something…"It's just—well, I'd have to think about it for a minute…" he said, awkwardly.

And suddenly he did think of it: Outside a gust of wind rose so quick and fast that it pulled the trees and rattled the french windows in their panes, through which an elegant woman's hat was seen to blow clean off, causing her to shriek so loudly that her cry could be heard in-doors. At the same moment a situation rose in Bark's imagination that was so large and intangible he could not grasp it. He saw himself caught in something from which there could be no returning. Something in the woman's gentle gaze presented itself to him suddenly like a foreign language, which he neither recognized nor understood. He could not imagine a man coming home after a year of war only to find his beautiful (for how could he deny it now?)—his beautiful wife sitting in a hotel lobby with a close personal friend without imagining a scene of horrendous violence ensuing. Of course it would drive a man to...well, to murder, he thought. He looked out of the hotel window and seemed to see another version of himself across the street, coffined behind the window of the café, pounding on the glass in fury and outrage, howling something incoherent about a wife, a family, a reputation to uphold at Briggman and Floss, to come back before it was too late.

"He should be here soon," she said, looking at her watch. "It's nearly quarter past. He's always right on time."

"Quarter past!" Bark shrieked, loudly and reflexively. He looked down at his watch and stood up in same motion, setting down his drink. Then he raised his head mechanically and looked out the window. Across the street, he located a man dressed in a loud green windbreaker, bent in the act of tying his shoe. He pointed mechanically and said "There he is!"

"Who?" the woman said, turning her eyes.

"My appointment!" he lied. "I'm terribly sorry—" the man called Bark said. "But I'm afraid I'll have to meet your husband another time. I simply must catch this man."

"But what man?" she said. "I don't see anyone."

He was gone before she could even finish her question. He burst out of the doors, clutching his brief-case under his arm and was nearly hit by a car entering the street. The wind caught him crosswise and nearly took away what was left of his breath. He ran like a thing pursued across the street and into the café where Sandra, his dependable waitress greeted him by saying, "Hello Mr. Barkley—forget something?"

"I'll have the next available table," he panted with his characteristic brusqueness.

"We've got one there by the window if that's alright?"

He resumed his seat. The young women he had seen sitting there from the hotel a moment earlier had moved to a booth further in, probably on account of the sunlight, he guessed, which, at that precise location and hour, was exuberant and overwhelming. He tried to look across the street at the french windows to see whether a woman was still sitting there, but he only saw his own squinting face, which seemed sad, old, and in this season, which he had begun to think of as completely absurd—hopelessly alone.

"Get you a coffee, Mr. Barkley?" Sandra asked him.

"No—ice water will be fine," he stated, pulling out a file from his brief-case which had the name BROWN written on it. He took out his cell phone and dialed a number.

As Sandra set down his water and straw she heard him say into the receiver: "I'd like you to cancel my appointments for this afternoon. That's right—all of them."

Just then a swath of clouds formed a canopy over the sky. In the ensuing shade, the man called Bark perceived from his station a man and a woman exiting the hotel. The woman was beautiful; the man looked like he was cut from bronze. They seemed to be arguing, walking away down the sidewalk towards something he could not predict.

Sandra waited for him to hang up, though she could see his call had long been over, then said: "Get you anything else, Mr. Barkley." It was not even a question.

He did not look at her. "There's just no reaching some people," he said.

A Plot to End It
Sam Steffen

I

John Runner had nearly given up hope of ever being free of Aida Holmes when the idea came to him to buy a ring.

"Wedding or engagement?" the jeweler had asked.

"Wedding," John said.

"Very good, sir," said the jeweler, who was bald and had a thin orange mustache about the length and width of his two orange eyebrows. "Would you care to see our selection?"

"That won't be necessary," John said with confidence. "My darling and I are not the flashy sort. We don't need anything expensive. Just the plainest sort will do." He could have patted himself on the back for the word 'darling.' It betrayed nothing of his contempt for Aida.

"Very good, sir. If you'll just join me at the fitting table…"

John and Aida had been together for nearly a year. It was the longest he had ever been with a woman, and he was beginning to feel that if he did not do something drastic soon, he would wind up married to her, which, to John Runner, was tantamount to being entombed. "I'd sooner have a bullet in my brain than a ring on my finger," he told his pals at work, who were always jonesing him about tying the knot. John Runner did not believe in marriage. He believed in many things: ghosts, aliens, the undead—but not marriage. Marriage, for John Runner, fell into the categories of make-believe with which he also put nursery-rhymes, fairy-tales and religion. "Aw, cut it out with that!" he would yell over the sound of factory machines. "I'm not getting hitched. That's for kids!" Everyone he knew who had been married only wound up getting divorced as soon as they had children. Most of the people he worked with at the factory were divorced, and if they weren't currently—they would be soon, he could tell. It had happened to his parents and it had happened to their parents before them. He had seen it too many times to ever feel that he would fall victim to the same mistake himself.

John was a bachelor at heart. He had met Aida the same way he met all the girls he dated: at Ponzo's. Ponzo's was a bar in Capernaum, where John lived. He liked going there because he had been picked up there more than once by women he considered to be better than average-looking. In the past he had been fortunate, he felt, to find someone who was not looking for anything serious. His habit was to go alone on singles night, which was the first Friday of each month, and to sit at the bar and drink until he was noticed. This had worked well enough for him in the past and had always resulted in a drunken sexual escapade back at his apartment, followed by a hung-over breakfast in the morning and an impersonal good-bye. John did not mind that he had never had a serious relationship. For him the desire for romance was a feeling of the glands which came occasionally, at moments of extreme loneliness— and could be gotten rid of on the first Friday of the month, provided he played his cards right and did not drink too much too early. If anyone had asked him whether he had ever been in love, he might have said he fell in love every time he turned over the leaves of his calendar. In fact, he did not know anything about *real* love.

Aida Holmes knew about love. She knew that you did not fall in love at the sports-bar on singles night, that no matter how much you wanted it, no matter how open to its million manifestations you might be, *that* was not where you were going to find it—despite her friend Barbara's insistence. Barbara went to singles night on the first Friday of every month and averaged about three lays per year, which she boasted of almost constantly.

"But it doesn't mean anything to you," Aida would remind her.

"So?" Barbara would say, with a terrible rasp.

"Doesn't that bother you? Don't you want to share yourself with someone you can put your faith into—

someone you can be with for a long time—for more than a single night, anyway?"

"Eech," Barbara wretched. "Who wants that? I'm just looking for a good time. And God knows, you seem like you could use a good time, too."

Aida did not want to have a good time. She was only interested in love. She had been in love before, which is why she knew about it. She had loved a man named Peter Bangles who had played the French horn in a symphony orchestra, but they had broken up when his residency at the conservatory had expired. At first they had agreed to continue to date long-distance, but a month after he left, she had received a letter from him to the effect of their immediate and permanent termination as lovers. Shortly after that even their friendship dissolved. That had been nearly five years ago, when Aida had worked in the music library at the University. She and Peter had not spoken since, and she had not been on a date in all that time, and was now pushing thirty. Nowadays she kept the books for a small restaurant chain in Capernaum. She did not mind waiting for love; but Barbara, who was a waitress where Aida worked, thought that sounded juvenile and pathetic.

"You need to get over that old boyfriend of yours and realize he was probably sleeping around on you before he even had the heart to tell you."

"No," Aida said. "Peter wasn't like that. Peter was different."

"Honey," said Barbara. Her voice sounded old and cancerous. "I hate to break it to you, but they're all the same. In fact, one's so much like another that it don't matter whether you keep one around to treat you nice and one to screw you when you want it and one to give you children and one to help you raise em—they're all out huntin' the same thing in the same rotten race—it's just that they're all at different stops along the way."

"If that's how you see it," Aida said, "why do you care for any of them?"

"Because," Barbara coughed. "I'm a woman who knows what the score is, and I just want to have a good time while I can."

Aida did not understand why Barbara went to singles night. She was already seeing a man from Springfield named Harvey who probably loved her. Aida had watched them together at the restaurant— clinking glasses after her shift was over and laughing as they shared a plate of food. It reminded her of how she had been with Peter, so easy and care-free. It made her sick to her stomach to think that Barbara was not in it for anything more than...well, to think that Barbara had no *real* feelings for him.

"What about Harvey?" Aida would say.

"What about him? He's one of 'em, too."

"Nothing special?"

"Nothing special."

In the end it was love—not Barbara—that persuaded Aida to go to the bar. It was the only thing that could have persuaded her, when she had been so dead-set against it. One Friday after the doors of the restaurant had been closed and the dishes cleaned and the floors swept and the money counted and the books balanced, Barbara and Harvey had caught ahold of Aida, just as she was on her way out the door.

"Aida—" Barb said. "We're heading over to Ponzo's for singles night. Wanna come?"

"Are you allowed to go if you're a couple?" Aida asked, playfully.

"Oh—hush!" Barb said, waving her hand. "We're not breaking any laws."

"There's going to be a live band," Harvey said. He was a tall man, very young-looking. He exuded innocence, Aida thought, like an aftershave. The poor dear, she thought. "I think they're a jazz band."

"Really?" Aida said. The mention of jazz piqued her interest. She was a sucker for music—particularly jazz. Peter had played in a jazz band for a time...

"Yeah! C'mon, c'mon, c'mon—" Barbara hacked, literally grabbing Aida by the arm and pulling her along. "It'll be fun! Fun! Fun!"

"I'll have to take my own car," she said, reluctantly.

"Yes! Got her!" Barbara cried.

Aida had never been to Ponzo's, or to anything that was even remotely like Ponzo's. Her idea of a good time was going to a film at the independent movie theater and then going to a quiet café somewhere afterwards to discuss its merits and shortcomings over coffee and a biscotti. And while this was her idea of a good time, it was seldom that she could ever find anyone to accompany her to a movie, much less to the café afterwards for some sort of discussion. She hadn't gone to a movie unaccompanied since she had broken off with Peter, though she continued to go by herself on a weekly basis. Sometimes, buying her ticket or her popcorn, there was a small glowing coal of a hope in her that she might meet someone in the theater who had also come alone, who was intelligent and funny and handsome, whom she could talk about the film with afterwards and maybe—who knew— love? But there never was. Aida always got there early and sat in the back so she could see the faces of everyone else as they shuffled in. Usually people came in pairs, or as pre-established family units. It made her feel like she had a role to play, being the first one there and the last to leave—like she was the unofficial mother of the movie-house, and everyone there was somehow her responsibility. At least that's what she told herself, to keep herself from feeling overwhelmed by heartache and loneliness.

She did not see the appeal of going to a bar. She thought bars to be noisy, smoky places where you could not do much if you were not in a shouting mood, which Aida seldom was. Nor was she often in a dancing mood, or a smoking mood, or a dart-throwing mood, or a brawling mood, or a hard-drinking mood, or a vomiting mood, for that matter. She knew that there were people for whom a good bar was a like a second home—or even a first one; but she didn't know any of them. With the exception maybe of Barbara, for whom Ponzo's seemed a kind of whole world miniaturized into three dark rooms, where she met men and saw old friends and celebrated and mourned with them and fought and played and smoked and drank and sang and danced, and danced, and danced, and felt free; in short, where most of her non-work-related interactions with other people took place.

Aida did not think much of Barbara's way of life; she did not think much of Barbara when it really came down to it—but lately she had been given to reflecting at some length upon her own opinions of others because of a film she had seen which had had a profound effect upon her.

Even though she had seen it twice, and could still recall the plot to within some degree of detail, the name of the film had long eluded her. It had been a new release when she had seen it, had been shot in black-and-white, and was German, with English subtitles. The plot had concerned a prominent courtroom judge of good reputation in small Catholic municipality somewhere in Germany. Early on in the film, the judge's infant son dies of a rare form of cancer. While he is grieving, the judge is visited several times in his home by different priests who appear to be in a conspiracy to help him find the love of Jesus Christ. The judge, who is an atheist, demonstrates a cordial appreciation for their concern, but in the end does not take them up on any of their offers, and requests only to be left alone. His wish is granted. By a series of events, then, the judge is presented with a case involving some sort of embezzlement scandal in the church. As it turns out, some of the people being tried are the very priests who visited him in his home. Upon reflection, it occurs to him that they may have been trying to involve him in a scheme of theirs in order to blackmail him for his protection. This realization, which turns out to be fallacious, nevertheless arouses his anger, and when the verdict is reached, he passes a far harsher sentence upon the priests than anyone anticipates. As a result of his decision, many of the townspeople rise up in anger against him and eventualize his ejection from power. Following his dismissal, his wife divorces him and he becomes homeless and despondent.

After losing his family and his reputation, the judge discovers through one of the townspeople that the embezzlement scandal was not nearly as nefarious as it had seemed. Lacking any means of reversing his sentence, he decides to visit one of the priests in prison. The priest appears very glad to see him, and they engage in a short exchange in which the judge apologizes and explains that he is sorry but that there is nothing he can do now to reverse the wrong he has done. The priest forgives him instantly, tells him not to worry, that there is plenty of work for him to do in prison, and that if he has wound up there by an apparently unjust sentence, it is all in accordance with God's plan. The priest suggests that perhaps the judge has been sent to prison in order to minister to those who are in greater need. The judge is baffled by this response and becomes angry and demands to be given a task to perform by which he can make things right. The priest says that all is well, and that if he wishes to know what to do further, he need only ask the Lord God.

In the next scene of the film, the judge, dirty and disheveled, enters a cathedral and seats himself in the very last pew. There is no one else in the cathedral. He sits there uncomfortably for what feels like a long time. No music is playing. The scene is shot in such a way—with the camera following the judge into the church and remaining behind him the entire time, never cutting away to see his face or even to get a proper view of the interior of the church—that Aida forgot, just for a moment—for the duration of the scene—that she was in a movie theater. After a long while, there is a slight commotion at the front of the church, and a man appears exiting a doorway and walks hurriedly down the aisle, crossing himself before exiting the church altogether. The man does not look at the judge as he passes, but the judge turns around in his pew to watch the man leave, at which point the audience catches a glimpse of his face and it is evident that he has been weeping, noiselessly. When the sound of the door closing ceases and the silence returns, the judge rises timidly and, as if he cannot decide whether to remain or depart, walks with extreme hesitation towards the front of the church. The camera does not follow him, or cut away, but remains fixed where it is at the back of the church, pointing indiscriminately forward, so that as the judge walks towards the dais, he appears to grow smaller. He grows smaller and smaller until he is a miniscule, dark, far-away shape at the front of the church, where he enters a doorway and disappears altogether. And still the camera does not cut away. The audience remains at the back of the empty church, looking down the aisle over the pews at the barely recognizable crucifix at the front while the audio presents the sound of a man sobbing. The sobbing goes on for some time before a stranger's voice says in German, and the subtitles appear in bright white at the bottom of the screen:

"What is your confession, my son?"

"Forgive me," the judge's voice-over says. "Forgive me. I made a mistake."

"What is your sin, my son?"

"A mistake," he says. "I convicted an innocent man. A man of the cloth. I sentenced him to eleven years in prison because I thought it was what was just. I know now that I was wrong. I made a mistake. I visited him in prison to ask him to forgive me and he said I was absolved. He said I must ask the Lord to be forgiven."

"How long since your last confession, my son?"

At this point the camera cuts to the judge's tear-streaked face in the confessional. He is sobbing.

"Never. I've never done this. I'm not a Catholic. I don't believe in God."

There is a long moment of silence, for which the judge appears to be listening intensely.

"Father?" the judge says.

"Yes, my son?"

"What am I to do?" he says. "I want to be forgiven."

"Have you accepted the Lord Jesus Christ as your

own personal Lord and Savior, who was divinely conceived and died upon the cross in order to save—"

"No!" he says. "I don't believe all that—I don't believe it! I don't believe!"

"Are you familiar with the Holy Scripture, my son?" the confessor asks.

"Parts of it. What they made us read in school."

"Are you familiar with gospel according to Matthew, the seventh chapter, verse one?"

"No," says the judge. There is another long silence. "Father!" the judge says with impatience. "Father!"

"Yes, my son?"

"What does it say? What does it say, dammit!"

"I suggest you read it for yourself."

It is worth mentioning here that the scene is particularly resonant insofar as it is no doubt intended to echo the earlier court-room scene in which the judge passes sentence upon the priests. Before bringing down his gavel, he asks one of the priests if he is familiar with an obscure court case which he names in reference to his decision. The priest says he is not familiar with the case, to which the judge says, with extreme condescension, "I suggest you read it for yourself."

Hearing his own words being thrown back at him, the judge becomes outraged and bursts out of the confessional. He storms to the nearest pew where he pulls a bible out and opens it to the relevant page.

He reads silently for a time and falls down into the pew, apparently preoccupied in some deep personal reflection. He begins to sob again and while he is crying says desperately:

"But it's impossible! Impossible! It can't be!"

In a fit of anger, the judge returns to the confessional where he tears the curtain on the father's side. To his amazement, there is no one in the booth.

"Father?" he says. He enters the booth, apparently searching for a secret exit or escape hatch, but there is none. "Father? But...but...I don't understand. It is impossible. Impossible!"

The first time she had seen the film, Aida had left the theater feeling confused about the film's message, if it had one. She was not familiar with the bible, herself, and she decided that part of her confusion had to do with the fact that the film had made no effort to provide for the audience the passage of scripture which the confessor had suggested the judge read. Upon exiting the theater with the other members of the audience, she overheard an older woman say to an older man, "So what was the passage?"

The man responded by saying, "Who knows? Who cares? Probably a lot of mumbo-jumbo. I need to piss."

It made Aida long for Peter, who she was sure

would have known what the passage was, if only for the familiarity with holy scripture that his love of classical music had no doubt bred into him. Peter had been wonderfully well-rounded, and demonstrated an incredible understanding of subjects Aida knew little or nothing about. She decided she would look it up.

When she returned home that evening, she had looked high and low for her Bible, which she could have sworn upon a stack of Bibles that she had owned at one point—but she had either misplaced it or thrown it away accidentally, as she could not find it anywhere. She recalled that when she had been confirmed at St. Mary's at the age of thirteen, everyone in her confirmation class had received a bible and a gold necklace from which a small cross depended. Afterwards her parents had told her that she was old enough and far enough along on her faith journey to decide for herself whether going to church was something she wished to continue doing.

"You mean I don't have to go anymore?" she had said, with excitement.

"What your mother and I mean," her father had said, "is that we're no longer going to make that decision for you."

She had not been inside a church since. While she was searching her bookshelves, it occurred to her that even if she found it, she would not necessarily know what passage to look for. Believing as she did when the passage was mentioned in the film that it would be provided for the benefit of the audience, Aida made no effort to remember either the chapter or the verse number. She recalled only that it was somewhere in the book of Matthew. She wondered, as she sought the holy book, whether she would even know where to find that.

Aida's lack of understanding of the end of the film, followed by the startling discovery that her household was apparently dispossessed of the book that might have clarified it (and which, even identifying as non-religious as she did, she nevertheless believed wholeheartedly that no household ought to be without)—promoted in Aida the desire to see the film a second time. The next day was a Saturday, and on her way to the independent movie theater she had stopped into a small bookstore and bought the smallest, cheapest Bible she could find, which had cost her a whopping sixty-five dollars. When the bookseller had rung it up for her, she had nearly reconsidered.

"Sixty-five dollars!" Aida exclaimed. "I hope I've got enough left for the movies," she said, ruffling through her purse.

"Funny, isn't it?" the cashier said.

"What's funny about sixty-five dollars?" Aida asked.

"Dunno," said the bookseller. "Just that a book that says 'If thou wilt be perfect, go and do away with all thou hast,' should cost so much."

"Does it really say that?" Aida said.

"Yes, ma'am," said the bookseller.

She handed him the money and he counted it and rang it up. "It says a lot of things."

"Yeah?" Aida said. She nearly told him that she was buying it so she could better understand a foreign film—but she decided against it.

"Oh, yes," said the bookseller. He was an aging man with spectacles that slanted down on the end of his nose. From the way he was typing on the register he seemed the sort of person for whom technology was more a burden than a tool. "It also says, 'It is easier for a camel to pass through the eye of a needle than it is for a rich man to enter the kingdom of heaven.'"

"You don't say," said Aida.

"Yes, ma'am. Matthew chapter nineteen, verse... ah, let me think...twenty-four, I believe."

She had begun to feel uncomfortable, waiting for her change.

"You can look that up, if you don't believe me."

"I believe you," Aida said.

"You probably knew that one yourself, didn't you?"

Aida stared at the man, who was smiling at her,

taking his grandfatherly time in making change for the eighty dollars she had given him. She did not know what to say.

"Say," said the man. "What's a girl like you doing buying a Bible for anyway? Don't you have one? It's a book no home ought to be without, you know."

"I know," Aida said, almost ashamedly. "I've got one. This one's a gift," she lied. "For my niece."

"Well—that's nice," the man said, handing her her change. He looked as if he was about to say something else, but Aida quickly left the shop.

She walked two more blocks to the movie theater and paid for her ticket and took her seat in the back of the auditorium, as usual. She was twenty minutes early. While she was waiting for the movie to start, she opened her bible and began to read it. She found the book of Matthew in the index, and started there. When the lights went down she closed the book, but kept her finger in the pages. When the scene came where the judge is told by the priest what passage to consult, Aida flipped to it in her own bible and read the impossibly small letters by the glowing light of the film-screen.

"But it's impossible! Impossible! It can't be!" the subtitles read upon the screen.

After reading the passage she set down the book and began to watch the remainder of the film with understanding.

Following her second viewing of the film, Aida floated to her favorite café where she always ordered a coffee and a biscotti. While awaiting her coffee, she entertained herself with wondering, as the judge in the film had, whether it was truly possible to live one's life without ever forming any sort of judgment of another person. From her seat in the café, she looked out at the bookstore across the way to where she had purchased her Bible and thought of the bookseller. She thought of how distastefully he had treated her and how presumptuous he had been to ask about what she was doing buying a Bible. What business was it of his? She wondered what it would feel like to have had an exchange of the sort she had had and to come away feeling unaffected. She thought of all the people in her life and what her opinions of them were. She thought of her mother and her father. She thought of Peter Bangles. She wondered whether she had a nobler opinion of him than she ought to. She thought of her bosses and co-workers, her friends from college and high-school, the people she liked as well as the people she despised. As she thought of them, she thought that many of her opinions of others were based upon her own opinion of their opinions of her, of which, she realized, she could never be entirely sure. The following weekend she stifled her reservations about both Barbara and Harvey and accompanied them to Ponzo's where she met and fell in love with John Runner, a man with whom she had almost nothing in common.

II

John Runner sat at the airport at a quarter to midnight with his tickets and no luggage and waited to be called to board. He had never been on a plane before, and was afraid of flying—but not nearly as afraid as he was of being married. There is no fear that cannot be overcome in service to one greater: if not for his plan, John was sure it would have already happened.

It had taken him a long time to make it through security where he had been forced to throw away a pocket-knife his grandfather had given him before he had passed away, which John had carried with him ever since and which the old man had told John to keep always so that he could pass it on to his own children someday. When the security guard pulled him aside and informed him that he would not be allowed through unless he parted with his knife, John said, "Alright—," and thought: I ain't gonna be havin kids anytime soon anyway—what do I need that old thing for? "Do you need my wedding ring, too?" he sarcastically added, pulling it off of his finger and holding it out like an offering in his palm. The security guard shook his head and waved him through. A morbid thought touched his spite then and he hoped, for a fleeting moment, that his plane would crash somewhere in the Midwest, and that there would be no survivors.

"Attention valued customers—at this time we will begin boarding flight 4559 with service to Chicago."

John looked at his tickets. This was it. He did not know what the protocol was. He looked all around him. Nobody rose or seemed to even care that the announcement had been made. He looked over at a pale elderly man sitting next to him who was calmly reading a newspaper and said, rather urgently, "Is this us? Do we get on now?"

The man looked at him strangely, and closed his paper. "Where you heading?"

"Las Vegas," John said.

"Vegas?" the man said. "No kidding. Well ain't that something?"

"Are we supposed to get on?" John said.

"Are you sure you're at the right gate?" the man said. "This flight here's going to Chicago."

John looked at his tickets.

"Well—I've got two. It says I'm going to Chicago first, then on to Las Vegas."

The loudspeaker said: "At this time we would invite any passengers requiring the use of a wheelchair or any of our handicap services to please come forward."

"What does that mean?" John said.

The man took his ticket and looked at it. He pointed at number and said, "You see this here? This is your boarding section. When they say 'Now boarding zone 4 passengers,' that'll be your turn."

"Okay," John said. He sat back in his seat, looking around at all the other people with their bags and suitcases. He thought they looked sort of like prisoners, chained to heavy things that would prevent them from making an easy getaway if they ever needed to. He pitied them.

"This your first time flying?" the man said.

"Yeah," John said, easily. Then a troubling thought occurred to him and he said, "Well, actually no. I've flown lots of times. I just haven't done it in a while's all."

He turned away from the man to signify that he had all the information he needed and that he didn't appreciate all the questions. The man leaned over and said: "Say, you wouldn't happen to be a—gambling man, by any chance, would you?"

John looked at him stonily.

"You said you were going to Vegas," the man said.

"Oh—yeah. No. That's where I'm going, but I ain't no sort of gambler."

"You mind if I ask what brings you out there?"

John minded. He actually minded a lot. But he had prepared an answer for just such an occasion as this. "A buddy of mine's getting married," he said. "I'm supposed to be in his wedding. Just going out for the weekend, then right on back."

"Good place for a wedding," the old man said, and laughed.

Up until now John had thought the man to be friendly enough. But something about his laughter hurt John's pride. He decided that he was an enemy and could not be trusted.

The loudspeaker said: "At this time we would invite any first-class passengers and any of our preferred rewards members to please begin boarding."

At this announcement the man got up. John watched him stuff his newspaper into his brief-case and put on his hat and coat. He then reached into his shirt-pocket and produced a card which he passed to John. It said:

TABLE 157
SANDS CASINO

The man said, "Not that it's any of my business, but I've been to Vegas enough times to know that anybody travelling to Vegas in your condition— without luggage, I mean—isn't just going for the ceremony. Now I don't know you and I don't know what you're in for, or what you've put up or what you've lost, but I'm a man who likes it when the odds are slim. Your running into me here in

Philadelphia when you've got another plane to catch and I've got two before we wind up in the same place—now that's a long shot. Tell you what: I don't know what your game is, but when you're all through with whatever your *real* business is, if you want to take a real chance—a *big* chance—you come see me. That's where I'll be. Safe travels." He raised his hat a little and made a slight bow and then quickly walked over to the main gate where his ticket was scanned and he was ushered without resistance onto the plane. John stood aghast.

"At this time, we would invite any zone 2 passengers to please form an orderly line and begin boarding."

John continued to sway where he was as he watched the people congregate in a rather disorderly fashion, presenting their tickets at the gate before being ushered aboard. Out in the main thoroughfare of the airport, people were moving at various paces and speeds. There were people standing around, people walking, and occasionally people sprinting for dear life, as though pursued. He felt a deep anger rising in him. Behind him a woman was talking rather loudly on the telephone with someone.

"No—I love you more," she was saying. "No—I love *you* more."

John wanted to tell the woman to shut up. He wanted to tell her that nobody wanted to hear about her stupid romance, that this was a public place, for Chrissake—and didn't she have any consideration for others. "No—I *love* you more. Okay, seriously, though. We're just boarding now. I'll call you when we land. Love you."

The thought of Aida collided with John then like a passenger hurrying to catch a plane. He felt a pang of remorse for what he was doing. He had not told her where he was going or for how long he would be gone. He had visited the jeweler's right after work, had come to the bus-station right from the jeweler's, had ridden almost two hours to get to Philadelphia International and was now on his way to Las Vegas, by way of Chicago, where he hoped to gather enough evidence against himself that Aida would be forced to leave him. He promised himself when he put on the ring that he would not call her, that he would not answer his phone if she tried to call him, that he would see this plan through this time.

Of course, he had made similar promises in the past. There had been dozens of previous plans to break it off with Aida—John had been honest, he had lied; he had tried reasoning with her, he had tried feigning insanity; he had ignored her, he had smothered her; he had treated her unfairly and discredited her; he had insulted her and berated her; he mocked and slandered her; he had on numerous occasions tried to get her fired from her job; he had tried to embarrass her in public; he had made a fool of himself regularly in front of her parents; he had refused to bathe or maintain his appearances; he had put on weight; he had grown unsightly facial hair; he had tried to be caught cheating on her; he had even gone so far as to threaten to commit suicide—nothing had worked. In every instance she had called his bluff or forgiven him, had twisted his intention around into something it wasn't, had complimented his strengths in light of his shortcomings and found a way to perceive his meannesses as subtle gestures of charity for which she could ultimately express her earnest gratitude. The only thing he hadn't done was forcibly beat and kill her, but these were things John Runner was constitutionally incapable of doing—of even imagining doing—to a woman, no matter how badly he wanted to get away. Still, it was the only thing he had wanted for some time—to be free of any and all attachment—and he had never imagined that anyone could hang on to someone like him the way Aida Holmes had hung on. In her, John believed he had found, much to his misfortune, someone who would love him no matter how hard or how little he tried to love her back—that is, unconditionally. And how else—John thought for the thousandth time as he stood up with his duffel bag to board his first plane—how else could you be rid and free of someone who loved you without conditions, except by marrying somebody else, preferably a stranger of no importance, in an all-night drive-through-church on a drunken binge in the natural course of a spur-of-the-moment trip to Las Vegas? Yes— without going into too much detail, this was the entirety of his plan. He had already purchased the ring; he only needed to go through the motions of flying to Vegas in order to procure a marriage license and an alibi. Then he could come back and tell her whatever he wanted. He could tell her that he was in love with another woman and she would have to know it by the metal on his hand. He would be free. After this weekend, he thought. He wondered, as he stared shamefully down at his ticket and was shuffled slowly towards the mouth of the widening gate, whether, in all of the millions of people who were at that very moment in some sort of transit, there was anybody traveling with motivations even half as shallow, conceited, and despicable as his own.

III

There had not been any live jazz band at Ponzo's that night like Harvey had told her there would be, and Aida might have left sooner than she did had it not been for the fact that the jukebox was also broken. Ponzo's was a dark bar, and setting foot inside on singles night, one could tell that it was a popular meeting-place for lots of unattached people: the tables and chairs had been pushed aside and were stacked carelessly atop one another for the purpose of allowing a dance-floor, above which streamers and colorful Christmas-tree lights had been hung, along with an enormous banner that designated the space as belonging to SINGLES ONLY. What seemed like an enormous number of people were standing around in the clearing, talking loudly so that they sounded like an audience of some-kind, waiting for a show to start. In the far corner of the room it looked like a fight of some kind was erupting. Over the din of conversing voices, someone was shouting, "Ponzo! Ponzo! Where's the music?" while on the floor behind the flashing juke-box which had been scooted away from its restingplace against the far wall, a man lay on his back with a small flashlight in his mouth, his hands buried in wires.

Aida walked in the wake of Barbara, who knew just about everybody in the place. All the while she felt her heart casting judgment upon the people she saw. *Roughneck. Raised in a broken home. Womanizer.* She could not help it. It occurred to her that casting judgment every now and again was a mechanism of defense, a way of protecting yourself from others who might come to do you harm. If you could not detect a bad seed when you saw one, she thought to herself…but before she could even finish the thought, she was being introduced to John.

"I want you to meet a friend of mine," said Barbara. "Aida, this is John. John, this is my good friend Aida. She works with me over at the restaurant."

"Pleasure," Aida said.

John nodded.

"John's not much of a dancer, either," Barb said, looking at Aida. Then she looked back at John and said, "This is Aida's first time at a single's night."

"Oh yeah?" John said, indifferently. "Never been single before?" There was an empty glass in front of him and he looked to be about half way finished with another.

Aida blushed. "It's not that. I guess I just never really thought of it as a condition to celebrate."

John shrugged his shoulders without saying anything and looked again into his drink. For a moment the sounds of the bar seemed to wash over them like a crashing wave from the sea.

"To me, anyway," she said.

"Hey Harv," Barb called down the bar. "You gonna buy me a drink or what? Harv! Harvey!"

Aida felt uncomfortable. She decided if she was going to leave she was going to need a good excuse. She thought of telling them that she had forgotten something at the restaurant, and had to go back.

"John's one of the regulars here," Barb said to Aida. "He drives a forklift. And he's double-jointed."

"Really," Aida said, distantly.

"Well, Barb," John said. "It appears you know everything there is to know about me."

"Show Aida your double-joint," Barb said.

"No, thanks," said John.

"Come on. Please? Show her that thing you can do."

"No."

"Please?"

"No."

"Well," said Barb. "It's really quite something."

"I'll bet it is," said Aida.

"It's not," said John. "Barb's just making talk."

"Don't get me started," Barb said. "I could tell some stories."

"Well tell them already, why don't you," John prompted.

"You'd like that wouldn't you? I bet you would like that wouldn't you?"

"Leave it to you to tell me what I would and wouldn't like," John said.

Aida suddenly began to feel like John and Barbara had some kind of a history together. She could not tell if they were fighting or just kidding around. She did not know why Barbara was introducing them. Perhaps he had been one of the ones that she had boasted about and she had expected her to remember. "Is there a bathroom somewhere?" Aida said.

"It's in the back," Barb said. "Harvey—are you going to buy me a drink?"

The bathrooms at Ponzo's were old wooden single-toilet affairs whose walls were thoroughly graffitied and whose doors had lost their labels and their locks. Going in, she had been unable to tell whether she was using the men's room or the women's but decided it didn't matter and went in to one of them and shut the door and tried to lock it but couldn't and then stared at herself in the mirror until she began to sob. She had not expected to; it just happened. She had a feeling that she had to get away and then when she was alone it all came crashing down on her. She was thirty-one years old and did not know what she wanted. That is, she knew that she wanted those things in her life which she had had once and lost, which she knew she could not have again now. She wanted to be younger than she was, not to know what a struggle life was, to be happy. She wanted to be with Peter Bangles, to have married him. She felt certain that she had been happy with him and that she would have remained so if they only could have stayed together. She longed for some chance to go back in time, to do it all again and to get it right this time; she felt certain she would do things differently if she had only known then what a struggle it would be. She did not want to have to come to a place that had been designated for single people in order to find love. The thought of it depressed her to no end.

As she wept, her eye wandered to the graffiti upon the walls where she caught sight of the name 'Barbara' etched into a heart with the name 'Jose.' She looked for a long time at several obscene drawings which made her think that she was in the men's room, then at several more which caused her to strike that idea from her mind. She read long declarative sentences that were intended to slander and discredit and miniaturize their subjects, anonymous judgments that were published here for anyone and everyone to read. She thought again of the movie she had seen and felt the expense and weight of the bible in her purse. She read the telephone numbers of several people whom she could call "for a good time" and the addresses of several places she could go for the same thing. When she thought of how little she wanted to "have a good time," she began to sob afresh and was still crying when a loud and urgent knocking fell upon the door.

"Just a minute," Aida said.

She tried to catch her breath and wiped her cheeks with paper towels and blew her nose and threw the towels in the toilet and flushed them. While the water was still running, she opened the door. "Sorry," she said, instinctively.

She would tell him later on his own prompting, many months from now, in the course of one of their many fights, with neither regret nor shame but with a sincerity that would still cause her to cry as she explained it and a conviction he would find it practically impossible to counter or deny—that it had been here, as she had emerged from the bathroom at Ponzo's with tears in her eyes the night of their meeting and he had been standing there with a genuine expression of concern upon his face for her, that she had felt the first inkling of real, deep love for John Runner. "You asked me if I was alright and then you asked me why I was crying. And you looked...scared. You looked like you were about to break apart and I was the one who was crying. You didn't even know me. You didn't know anything about me. But you couldn't have made it any clearer if you had come out and told me you loved me right then and there."

"I don't love you," he would say. "I didn't then and I don't now. I don't love anybody. That wasn't love. I had to use the pot and you were in it."

"No," Aida would say. "It was love. Even if you don't know it. Even if you think it was something else. I know it was."

IV

It was nearly 1 a.m. when John arrived at the Las Vegas Airport. All he could think about was finding a hotel—cheap, but not too cheap—where he could get some rest. Funny, he thought—but all he really wanted out of his life anymore, when he really thought about it, was to feel again that he was well-rested. He had always thought as a young man that by the time he had reached the age of thirty he would have had all sorts of aspirations for a beautiful wife, a big house, children, perhaps a higher-paying job that would help him afford all of it, and that short of having any of them, he would be working his damndest towards obtaining what he lacked. But now that he was older, he realized that desire—his or anyone else's—had little or nothing to do with it; that marriage, children, divorce-alimony and taxable property were the things that came to you whether you wanted them or not. You could no more live free of any of them than you could board an airplane without a ticket. It might as well have been a law. What John wanted more than he wanted the unconditional love of a faithful woman or expensive items that would enhance and ensure a comfortable existence was a long draught of a good night's rest.

John had tried sleeping on both planes, but had had a miserable time of it. On his first flight, he had found himself seated next to a man named Lucas P. Conrad who introduced himself as the attorney he was and then proceeded without hesitation to interrogate John until they were well over Ohio.

"So who's getting married, then?"

"A friend."

"You the best man?"

"No."

"When's the last time you saw each other?"

"Couldn't say."

"It gonna be a big one?"

"Probably."

"Bachelor party and everything?"

"Probably."

"Where's it all happening?"

"I don't know."

"Well didn't you get an invitation?"

"Yes."

"Well what'd it say on there?"

"Can't remember."

"Is it at one of the casinos or a hotel or what?"

"I don't remember. Yeah."

John felt ashamed talking to the man, making up the story as he went along. It made him feel like he had committed a crime of some kind. While he spoke he kept twisting the ring on his finger, as though it had begun to cause an allergic reaction on his skin.

"Say—your wife going with you?" said the attorney.

"What?" John said. He let go his ring and made his hands into fists.

"That thing on too tight or what?"

"What?"

"That ring there. How long you been hitched?"

"Oh, a little while."

"Where's your wife?"

John felt his anger begin to rise. He resisted the compulsion to be truthful and explain that in the first place, she wasn't his wife, and in the second place, it was no business of his—but then decided it would be easier to say that she was at home. But his words seemed caught on the unfathomable idea that Aida Holmes would ever be his wife. "She's dead," he said.

"No—" said Conrad, looking deeply concerned.

"Yeah," John said.

"How long?" said Conrad.

"Oh, a little while now."

"My God. I'm terribly sorry. That's a terrible thing. And you still wear the ring...?"

John held out his hand and looked at it with curiosity. He thought it looked ridiculous and smiled a little. "Yup," he said.

"What happened?" the attorney said.

John sighed, trying to think of something to say. "I don't really feel like telling it," John said.

"That's alright," said the attorney. "That's okay. Boy, I understand. I really do. Still too soon. I know just what you mean, fella. Lost my wife a few years back, myself. Got cancer. Came up real quick. They didn't even catch it until it was in the third stage. Not a whole lot you can do at that point except brace yourself for the end." While the attorney said this he pulled out a fresh white handkerchief from his suit-pocket and wiped his brow with it, which was perspiring profusely. The flight attendants, at this point, were pushing their carts up the aisle, asking the passengers if they wanted food or a beverage.

"Say, can I buy you a drink, friend? When they get to us?"

John's heart sank. "No thanks," he said. "That's okay. I'm on the wagon these days."

"Boy—you're in recovery for that, too. Well, damned if you ain't one of the stronger among us. I'm in for all they've got."

Conrad watched the flight attendant intently for a moment, until she turned to him and asked him what he wanted. He ordered a double whiskey. She did not even ask John if he wanted a drink because he had turned his head towards the window and pretended to be fast asleep. He remained that way, wide awake with his eyes closed, thinking many troublesome thoughts, until he felt the wheels of the plane touch the runway in Chicago O'Hare. When the lights came on, Mr. Conrad stood up and retrieved his bag from the overhead. While he waited to deplane, he made sure to give John his card. "It was a pleasure meeting you, Mr..."

Mr. Conrad waited for John to tell him his name, but he didn't. "Nice to meet you, too," he said.

"If you ever get into any sort of legal trouble or anything like that—you give me a call. I know we're not exactly in the same jurisdiction, but I've been known to go out of my way for a friend. Matter of fact, that's what I'm doing here."

"I'll do that," John said, and he put the card in his pocket with the card from the gambler and his ticket.

"You hang in there," Conrad said solemnly, and then it was his turn to use the aisle, and he was gone.

On the second flight, John had also intended to sleep, but found himself in the aisle seat, beside a woman he considered to be uncommonly attractive, who smelled very pleasant and was very flirtatious. When John sat down she was talking to the passenger in the window-seat, and the two were laughing as if they were old friends. As soon as John sat down, he fastened his seat belt, and by the time it was on she had turned to him and was extending her hand towards him.

"Hi there," she said. "I'm Destiny." There was a tired, laid-back look in her eyes, that made John feel like she was deriving some sort of pleasure, just from looking at him.

"John," John said, coolly.

"John," she repeated. "I like that name. And what brings you to Las Vegas, John?" she said, interestedly. She spoke to him as though she wished to know everything about him, as though she intended to talk to him all the way to Vegas.

"What brings anyone to Vegas?" he said, playfully. "I'm just looking to have a good time."

"I'll drink to that," said Destiny, raising her delicate hand as though she were holding a glass of champagne. "You meeting your wife?" she said.

"What?" John said. He was perplexed by the frequency with which people seemed to notice his ring. He had presumed the institution marriage wore a subtler jewelry.

"Your ring, honey," she said, and she reached over and touched his hand, lifting it to him, as if showing him a part of himself he had never seen.

"Oh," he said. "That." He was somewhat aroused to hear her use such an affectionate term for him, and imagined himself kissing her. He thought that if he did, she would definitely be the most attractive woman he had ever kissed. He began to play with his ring, and made several subtle attempts to wiggle it off of his finger.

"Is your wife on the plane?" Destiny said, looking around.

"No," he said.

"Is she in Vegas, waiting for you?"

"No," he said.

"She's at home?"

"Yes," John said, ashamedly. Then he laughed.

"What's so funny?"

"Well…"

"What?"

"It's just that she's not there either."

"She's not at home?"

"No."

"Well where is she?"

"Nowhere," John said.

"She's nowhere?"

"I'm not actually married."

"Oh, really?" said Destiny, incredulously. "And what would your wife say about that?"

"No—It's true. It's kind of a funny story, actually."

"Is it?" Destiny giggled playfully. "Well—are you going to tell it?"

"I don't know. You'll probably think I just made it up."

"Will not," Destiny said.

"I mean it. It's a stretch."

"Try me."

"I don't know."

"Come on. Please? Look," she said. She threw her hair back over her shoulder, exposing her bosom more fully, and put her hand carefully over her breast. "I swear, cross my heart, whatever you tell me, I'll believe it."

"Well..." he said, smiling. He laughed for a minute privately to himself, slapping his forehead.

"What?" said Destiny.

"Nothing," he said, shaking his head.

"What? Are you making fun of me?" Destiny said. Her tone was entirely playful. She made him feel like they had known each other a long, long time. "Stop it," she said. "Stop laughing!"—and she swatted weakly at his arm.

"Oh, owch!" John said. "Careful! I just got a shot there!"

"Really?" said Destiny, looking sincerely afraid. "Oh, God. Sorry! I'm sorry. I didn't know—"

"No—I'm just kidding," John said.

Destiny laughed, and then swatted him harder in the same place. "You jerk!" she kidded. "Okay—maybe you're right. Maybe I won't believe you."

"Yeah," John said. "I'd better not tell it."

"Just tell it, already."

"Alright," John said. "Alright. So—a few months ago, a friend of mine got married."

"Oh, Jesus," Destiny said. "I can tell this is not going to end well."

"No, listen," John said, laughing. He could barely contain himself. He felt intoxicated all of a sudden, like he could have told her everything there was to tell, whether it was true or not. "It's not what you think."

"Okay. Go on. I'm listening."

"Alright. So a friend of mine got married a few months ago, and he wanted me to be in the wedding, right? He said, 'John,' he said, 'John—I need you, buddy. I need you to do me a solid and be one of my groomsmen. Only thing is,' he said, 'I need you to rent a tuxedo.' Said it wasn't his idea but his fiancé had this whole thing planned out in her head and she wanted it to be perfect. No screw-ups. Now I know you don't know me that well—we've only just met—but I'm not really the tuxedo-wearing type. If I ever get married—God forbid—I swear to God it's going to be in jeans and a t-shirt. Hell, I might just walk down the aisle barefoot if I want. I'm just...I just don't go in for that fancy stuff. That's not really me. Anyway. So I go in to see about renting one of these ensembles, and do you know how much it costs to rent a tuxedo? It's like a hundred fifty bucks or something ridiculous like that. So I went and got fitted and they told me how much it was going to be, and I just said, 'Hm—you know what? I just don't think this is for me.' I mean, it took them like two hours to take all these measurements and I just walked right out on them when they gave me that bill. So I called up my friend and I said, 'Carle— look man. You know I love you but I just don't think I can swing it. That's expensive, even for a wedding present.' And he was just begging me: 'Please, man. Do it for my wife.' He got down on his knees for his girlfriend, and he did the same for me just to get me into one of these penguin-suits. So I tell him I'll see what I can do. So I go around and I start asking everyone I know. The guys at the plant, the guys at the bar. I asked people I didn't even know. I asked my friggin mailman if he had a tux lying around."

"No you didn't," said Destiny, laughing.

"I did! I asked the UPS man. I say, 'Anybody got a tuxedo I could wear to wedding, or know anybody who does?' Nobody's got a clue. Tells you the sort of people in my life, don't it? Anyhow. So what ends up happening is word starts to get around that I need a tux. And one day I'm at the plant and I get called in by Kingsley, the boss-man himself. Guy's richer than God. He calls me into his office and I'm thinking I'm fired, right? Because the only time you get called in to the office is when you've either screwed up or you're getting promoted—and I know I wasn't getting no promotion. So they call me in and Kingsley's there and he says, 'Johnny,' like he's all friendly with me, all of a sudden. And I'm thinking, 'What the hell? This guy's never even met me. I don't know how he knows my name.' I'm thinking, 'Great—I'm canned.' But no: instead he says: 'I hear you're in need of a tuxedo.' And I'm confused at first, because I never said anything about this to any of the higher-ups. I don't exactly run in their circle, if you know what I mean. Well—it turns out, Kingsley, who's like the CEO of the company that owns the manufacturing plant that I've been working for the past ten years— turns out Stanley Kingsley is the grandfather-in-law of my buddy Carle's fiancé, if you can believe that. Turns out, my buddy Carle, who is a first-class knucklehead, is marrying into all kinds of money with this woman he's found. And this guy Kingsley wants to do his grand-niece a favor and get her dope of a grand-nephew-in-law's friend a tuxedo just so the wedding won't look asymmetrical. So he says: what's your size? And I'm like 'I don't know, sir.' And he walks up to me, and he tells me to stand up. And so I do. When a man that powerful says jump, you don't even think to say how high, you just do it. So I get up and I'm about to piss myself because this guy's just coming towards me and I don't know what he's going to do—if he's going to threaten me or kill me or what. We're alone in his office and he's got more money than I've ever heard of. And he walks right up to me, and I start to shake I'm so afraid.

And he comes right up to me like he's going to hug me and he looks right into my eyes and he holds his arms out like…I don't know. Like Christ. He's making this Christ-on-the-cross motion standing so close to me I can smell his old rich breath. And he says, 'Do like me.' So I put my arms out and we're just standing there looking at each other from an inch away and then he does this thing where he puts palms flat against mine and presses his chest against my chest and he's right level with me like he's going to kiss me. I'm just standing there turning blue because I'm not even breathing anymore."

Destiny laughed.

"And then he says, 'I think you're just my size.' And he walks over to this bureau which he has in his office, and he pulls out this hangar and says, 'Try this on.' So I figure he means right there in his office with him watching me and everything, so I drop trow and am practically naked before he says, 'Johnny! For Chrissakes—why don't you give yourself a little privacy and use the bathroom?'"

Destiny laughed at this, too. John felt pleased with himself, like he was telling a good story that might lead to more good times.

"So anyway. The guy gives me this tux from out of his personal bureau or whatever and he says, very casually, 'You can get that back to me when the wedding's through.' So that's that. I'm set. The wedding comes—I've got the tux. The wedding get's all screwed up anyway, but at least it's not my fault."

"What happened?" asked Destiny.

"Well—a lot of things. Some old jealous boyfriend of the bride's showed up right before things got going with a file he got from the DA's office on my buddy Carle that had a list of misdemeanors he'd been caught up in when he was a kid. Harmless stuff: bunch of DUI's, breaking an entering, urinating in public. You know, pretty trivial stuff. This guy worked for the justice department, I guess, and he came trying to break up the wedding and a couple of the other groomsmen caught wind of it before he could make too much of an intrusion. They took him out behind the church and beat the crap out of him right as the music's starting. They thought he was down and out but they didn't have time to tie him up or gag him or anything because they were missing their entering. So they bust in late, after the bridesmaids are all already up there, and they're all a little mussed and disheveled. And then Carle shows up, looking a bit pissed, and then Angela shows up and it's like everybody forgets everything. And then, after she makes this grand entering, this bozo from the DA's office comes in with a black eye and a bloody nose and a split lip and he just starts shouting in the church about what a criminal Carle is. Aw, it was a mess. There was a big brawl. It all got straightened out eventually—when they finally pulled everyone in Carle's extended family off of the guy, it was the bride who actually got him to leave. I don't know how, though. Probably had to tell him something he wanted to hear."

"That sounds pretty dramatic," Destiny said.

"Oh, it was. Aren't all weddings, though?"

"That still doesn't explain how you got that ring on your finger."

"Well, I'm coming to that," John said. "The thing that was interesting about this wedding, to me, I thought, was that…well, I should tell you. This guy made me angry—this ex-boyfriend of the bride's. He made everyone angry, but the thing about it was that he said some stuff about my buddy Carle that nobody who would call himself a friend would stand for without throwing a punch or two. And I wanted to: and I rushed at the guy, like everyone else did. But something happened when I was getting close to the guy and I saw him swinging at anyone and everyone. I remembered that I was wearing my boss's tux. And when I remembered that, it was like I felt this resistance that was deeper than anything I had ever felt, that just said, 'Don't do it. Not this time.' And I didn't. It was like having this expensive tux on that cost more than my life made me afraid to do anything too rash. It made me cautious like nothing else ever had. I ran towards him and then I ducked into one of the pews before I got too mixed in to the fight. I had to be careful. And I came away unscathed. But then—here's the kicker. So after all that drama, we go to this reception and there's this huge food-fight when they cut the cake. It started kind of small, where Carle shoved Angela's face in the cake, sort of playful-like, and then she swipes him with her slice, and then all hell breaks loose. And I couldn't avoid it. I was standing too close. I got covered in frosting—or, rather, my tux did. The tux that belonged to my boss. And it made me afraid for my life. So before I give it back to him, I decided I ought to take it to the cleaners and have it dry-cleaned."

Destiny seemed very pleased with everything John was telling her, and even though she was not saying much, she seemed to be listening very attentively, and reacting to almost every word.

"So then today," John said, "Today I go to pick up the tux and they said they were just finishing it up, it would still be about fifteen minutes. So I'm in this little shopping-center with a little time to kill, waiting to pick up this expensive tux, and I decide to just walk around for a few minutes. Right next door to the laundromat, there's a jeweler's. So I go into this jeweler's and I'm just looking around and then this guy comes up and starts asking me all these questions about my fiancé—which I don't even have. So he's yakkin away at me, and finally, just to shut him up, I ask the guy if I can try on this one ring. I don't know why. I guess I was just thinking about what it would be like to be married, you know? What it would feel like to have a ring—you know? Cause I've never worn one."

"You just wanted to see what it would feel like?" Destiny asked.

"I guess," John said.

"So you tried it on?"

"Yep. I put it on and wouldn't you know it—it got stuck."

"No," Destiny laughed.

"Yes. We were in there for an hour trying to get it off. Finally I told the guy I had to pick up my tux before the place closed, plus I had a plane to catch."

"So did you have to buy it?"

"What else could I do? I bought it and he said if I could somehow get it off in the next few days I could bring it back and he'd give me a refund."

"I don't believe it," Destiny said.

"See? I told you you wouldn't. And do you want to know what the real kicker is? The real kicker to the story is that if I had only rented my tuxedo it would've cost me a hundred and fifty bucks. For those jokers at the laundry place to get that cake out cost me two hundred and eight dollars, plus tax. Now isn't that something?"

"That is."

"I mean, you can't make this stuff up if you wanted to."

"No," said Destiny. "Life's like a big joke sometimes."

"Yeah," said John. "It sure is."

There was a moment where John seemed to be thinking of something else to say. He still could not believe he was sitting next to a beautiful woman, and having a wonderful time with her. It seemed too good to be true.

"Are you sure that ring is stuck, though?" Destiny asked. "Maybe, since we're at a higher altitude, it'll come off now. It'd be a shame to have to wear that all weekend."

"Oh, I'm pretty sure. Here. Go ahead," John said, passing her his hand. "Just try and pull this thing off."

Destiny took his hand gently and pulled weakly at the ring. Then she turned her back to him and set his hand in her armpit so that she was crushing it against the side of her breast. John almost couldn't bear it. He felt like she was teasing him, like she wanted him as badly as he wanted her. She moaned a little as she tried to force off the ring. John imagined what it would be like to be with her and was fantasizing heavily when suddenly he felt the ring slip off.

"Oh my God!" Destiny said, exuberantly. "It's off! I did it! Can you believe it!"

"Oh my God," John said, incredulously. "Thanks." He was actually shocked. The ring being off his finger made him think of Aida intensely, like she was there suddenly, sitting across the aisle from him, watching him, listening. He suddenly felt ashamed, like he would have to explain to Destiny that even though he was not married, he was still in a relationship from which he was incapable of severing himself.

"You don't have to thank me," Destiny said. "You just keep that in your pocket until you can get it back to the jeweler's." The way she said 'jeweler' made John think that she did not believe his story, like maybe she thought he was married in spite of everything he had just said.

"You know, you're pretty good at that."

"At what?" Destiny said.

"Is that the first time you ever pulled a ring off a man's finger?"

"Maybe," Destiny said, smiling. "Maybe not."

"Somehow I don't think it was."

"You know what they say about Las Vegas?"

"'What happens in Vegas…'"

She laughed. "Yeah—that's it."

"What about you?" John said.

"What about me?"

"What brings you to Las Vegas, of all places?"

"Same thing as you," she said. "Have a good time, do a couple shows, make a little something-something."

"Do you work in Vegas?" John said.

"Yeah. Sometimes."

"What do you do?"

"I'm a dancer," said Destiny.

"A dancer?"

"Yup."

"What kind of dancer? Ballet?" John said, kiddingly.

"No," Destiny laughed. "Try again."

"Let me think...flamenco?"

"Nope. Do you want a hint?"

"Sure," John said.

Destiny looked down at her bosom and placed her fingers along the inside of her brazier. She produced a card which she handed over to John. It was the third card he'd been handed in the last four hours. It read:

SPIRO'S GENTLEMAN'S CLUB
LAS VEGAS, NV
DESTINY

"That's where I work," Destiny said. "If you're looking to hang loose for a while, you should stop by. I dance there on the weekends."

"Thanks," John said. "Maybe I'll check it out."

"I'll be there tomorrow," she said.

"Perhaps I will, too," said John.

They had talked all the way through the flight, and were still talking even as they were walking off the plane, out the loading ramp, through the terminal. They had arrived. Other than his duffel bag, which contained a single change of clothes, John had no other luggage with him. As they walked towards the luggage retrieval area, following signs for the exit, Destiny told John that she was staying at the Crystal Ball Hotel and asked him if he had any arrangements. As much as he liked Destiny and wanted to see how far he could go with her, he did not like the sound of the Crystal Ball Hotel. It inspired a vision of a diamond chandelier beneath which he could imagine doling out hundreds of dollars on worthless expenses. Beyond this, he felt very tired all of a sudden, and very much wished to be alone. He told her he had made arrangements to meet a friend, and they parted ways. Before saying goodbye, she hugged him and told him in a sincere voice that it was nice to meet him, that she almost never met anyone nice on airplanes. Then she pulled his ear very close to her mouth and whispered, "If you want to call me, my number is on the back of that card." Then she walked away. As he watched her disappear beneath the bright lights of the airport, John wondered whether he would ever see her again. He decided that with a name like Destiny, the odds would have to be in his favor.

John hailed a cab from the loading zone and told the driver to take him to a cheap motel.

"Cheap? What is cheap? Who are you? What is cheap for you?" the driver asked.

"I don't know," said John. "Anywhere I can sleep for twenty bucks a night?"

"Twenty bucks?" the driver said. "No. Not in Las Vegas. You go back where you come from."

"Fifty?"

"A hundred is the cheapest," the driver said.

"Alright," said John. "Let's do that, then."

They sped off. As they drove John thought about how things would have been different if only it hadn't been for Aida. He felt that she was the reason he could not let himself be with a woman like Destiny. He believed, as so many men do who resign themselves to the love of a single partner and are miserable, that his unhappiness was caused by influences external to his own person and internal to those of another to whom he was close, and that if only he could be so lucky as to become free of his current circumstance, everything would change for the better. It was for this purpose that he had brought himself to Las Vegas this weekend. The more he thought of Aida, the more he hated her for making him fly all the way out here and then for preventing him from sleeping with Destiny—for this was the reason, after all, he told himself, that he had done the former and not the latter. It was all because of her. It did not occur to John that Destiny may have just been flirting; that she may not have been out to lay him as he flattered himself to think that she was. He believed wholeheartedly that if he had not had a girlfriend, who, even when he was not around her, still managed to penetrate his thoughts and act as a kind of conscience for him, he and Destiny would have already been kissing now, maybe in this very cab, speeding towards a hotel room in the heart of a city that swallowed all secrets, where there was a bed...and John would have been happy—blissfully happy.

He pulled out the ring from his pocket and put it back on his finger. As he did so, John briefly imagined the necessary confrontation that would ensue when he got back, and tried to decide whether, when he told Aida about Destiny, his trip, about everything—whether he would tell her that he had slept with her before they had gotten married. The grip of the ring around his finger seemed to cause a fresh wave of exhaustion to wash over him. He was tired, and wished that it could all be over.

V

It had been almost two weeks since Aida had seen or heard from John when she was awakened suddenly by a knocking at the door. It was very early, not yet even seven o'clock. Her alarm was set for seven-thirty. "It'll be John, thank God," she thought. She had not put anything on, and answered the door wearing only a nightgown. When she pulled the door open, she found it was not John, but a person whom she had never seen before.

"Are you Aida Holmes?" the person said. He was holding an umbrella high above a worn-looking hat, had leather gloves on and a long coat that went down to his shins.

"Um," Aida said. The sight of the man caused her no little surprise, and she took a stance that was more behind the door so that she could close it very quickly if she had to.

"Forgive me for calling so early," the man said, "but I'm afraid I have some rather unfortunate news."

"Who are you?"

"I'm inspector Trace," he said, touching the brim of his hat. "Pardon me. We've located your husband."

"My husband? But I don't have any husband."

"Oh?" the man said, looking very surprised. "Terribly sorry," he said. He produced a small sketch-book from his pocket upon which he had apparently scribbled some inaccurate notes. "Are you Aida Holmes?"

"Yes," she said.

"Is this 422 Constantine Street?" The address described John's apartment.

"It is."

"Do you live here with a Mr..." The inspector squinted at his notes but could not quite make out what he was trying to read. "Pardon me, a Mr.—"

"John," Aida gasped.

"Yes. That's the first name. Rumen? Rumen?"

"Runner," she said.

"Yes—is that what that says? Runner? Yes, I spose so." He produced a small pencil from his shirt pocket and crossed out the name and made another note immediately below it.

"Yes," Aida said, impatiently. "He lives here. This is his house. Have you found him? Do you know where he is?"

"Well it's rather unfortunate, Mrs. Runner," the inspector said. "You see—" he took a breath like he was about to tell her a very long story. "Actually, do you mind if I come in for a moment?"

"Where is he?" Aida said. She could feel tears welling in her eyes. "Tell me where John is."

"He's quite alright for the time being. It sounds like they've got him in a holding facility in Nevada, a small station near Las Vegas."

"Las Vegas?" Aida said. "What's he doing there? What's he doing there?"

"Well—it's rather a long story. It seems he was there to have a good time, gamble, throw away some money, you know. He's got himself into a bit of trouble, though."

"What sort of trouble?" Aida sniffled.

The inspector could detect a scene coming on. "Please," he said. "May I come in? It's a bit of a story."

"Just tell me here and then you can come in." Aida was beginning to cry. There was a cracking sound just now in her voice.

The man looked at the woman in the doorway and seemed to be considering his entire career choice. Then he sighed mightily. "Alright—well. I don't know how to tell you this, Mrs. Runner, but your husband—"

"He's not my husband," she said.

"Beg your pardon. Your 'John' has become involved in a murder case."

"Murder?"

"It would seem that while he was in Las Vegas, he and a young woman—" (the inspector looked at his notes as if to make sure the story he was telling was the correct one) "—it seems the two of them went into one of these all-night drive-through churches and got themselves married. There's a record there with both of their signatures. Someone named Jackie Rose? That name sound familiar to you at all?"

Aida shook her head. She did not believe anything she was hearing.

"One of the clerks there confirmed that's who it was. Then it seems they went back to some hotel room and spent the night there and at some point he murdered her in a fit of rage or passion. Strangled her. Tore one of her eyes out, too. Her body was discovered by one of the housekeepers and the investigation has led to your hus—I mean, John."

"That's wrong," Aida said, defiantly. "You've got the wrong man. Oh, no. Poor John."

"I'm told he was very sloppy about covering his tracks. He left his fingerprints everywhere—did it in his own hotel room, too. Of course, he was registered under a false name, but that hardly threw anybody. The police got to him before he even made it to the airport."

Aida looked at the inspector, but did not know what to say.

The inspector looked at his notes. "Oh yes," he said. "And he was wrapped up in some other criminal activities, as well, I'm told. You see, he had the telephone numbers of all these contacts on him at the time. One was a wealthy philanthropist. Another was a lawyer who's got a bit of a reputation for defending murderers. The story our team is putting together out there in Las Vegas would seem to indicate that the whole thing was premeditated, although there doesn't seem to be any previous connection between John and the woman he murdered. The motivations are still under investigation."

"I don't believe it," Aida said. "I won't. It's wrong. He didn't kill anyone. I know he didn't."

"I'm only telling you what I've been told," the inspector said. "Of course it's bound to turn up that nothing's as it seems. But the investigation's only just begun. And I haven't been out there myself, personally. I'm just the messenger in this case. It's a rather unfortunate position I'm put in, to tell you the truth."

Aida was too sad to say anything more. She was sobbing now, and looked like she was about to fall down. The inspector put his arms out as if to catch her, but she grabbed the door handle and then disappeared into the house. She did not close the door, only left it there, hanging open like a question she could not ask. The inspector stood in the doorway a moment, trying to decide what the best course of action would be, and whether any was necessary at all. Then, deciding that he had done his duty for the time being, that his work was finished, he shouted into the house: "Alright, Miss. I'll be going now. I thank you for your time. Call us at the station if you need anything." He touched his hat again, as if she were still standing there to see, and then pulled closed the door.

VI

John had spent the entirety of his first night in Las Vegas in his hotel room. The moment he entered the room, he hit the sheets and slept soundly, dreamlessly, and did not wake up until almost two o'clock the following day. It was Saturday. He got up and took one of the longest showers he could ever remember taking. By the time he was dressed again, in his only change of clothes, it was nearly three. Then he left his hotel room in search of a meal and a wife. The meal he found right across the four-lane road immediately outside his hotel. It was a steakhouse of some kind, where John was seated immediately and proceeded to order an enormous breakfast.

"Do you still serve breakfast?" he asked.

The waitress shrugged. "We don't really do breakfast. We do steak, ribs, porkchops…"

John looked at his waitress and wondered if she would want to marry him on a whim. He decided that she probably wouldn't.

"Alright," he said.

"Alright what?" she said.

"I'll take that."

"What?" she said.

"What you just said."

"Which? Steak, ribs or porkchop?"

"All of it. Just bring it all out."

The waitress looked at him. Then she wrote something on her pad. "You want something to drink?"

"I'll have a beer," John said.

"What kind?"

"Surprise me."

John did not finish even half of what he had ordered, but he drained his glass three times and was still waiting for his fourth beer when a waiter came over and set the bill on his table. He did not know what had happened to waitress, but he left his money on the table. When he returned to his hotel it was almost six o'clock. He decided that if he was going to find a wife he was going to have to be more proactive. He went to the front desk of the hotel and requested cab service to one of the casinos.

"Which casino?" the driver said over the sound of the engine running.

"I don't care. Any of them. Aren't they all in the same place?"

"Yes," the driver said. "But at one of them you will be lucky and at another you will be not-so-lucky."

"Well, which do you recommend if I'm the sort who wants to get lucky?"

"Come on. I'll take you."

He was taken to a casino called the Lucky-Strike. He wondered if the cab-driver was not employed by the casino to drive people there. When they pulled up, all the doormen seemed to know him.

"Hey Carlo!" they shouted to the cab-driver. "Brought another winner, I see? Very good! Mucho bueno!"

John thought they were probably all paid to say that sort of thing to each other. He did not mind. It made him feel good to have people believing in him for once, even if they had never seen him before and did not know what he was about. He entered the casino and started walking quickly around the room. John had never been inside a casino, and did not really know what he was supposed to do or where he was supposed to go. But he decided that if he looked like he did not know what he was doing, he would attract attention, which he didn't want. He only wanted to find a woman he could marry so he could go back to his hotel room and rest.

"Excuse me, sir?" a voice said.

John whirled around. A beautiful woman was standing there, smiling, with large dark eyes and long brown hair. "Yes?" he said. "Sorry."

"Do you need help with anything?" the woman

said. She was wearing a small hat with a red visor that looked like it was part of a uniform.

"I'm just looking for someone," he said. "No thanks."

He thought that she would leave him alone, but she hung on. "Who are you looking for?" she said.

"A wife," John said, and smiled.

"Your wife?" she said. "What does she look like?"

"I'm only kidding," John said. "I don't think she's here." He chuckled to himself.

The woman failed to see any humor in any of it. "Do you want a drink while you wait?" she offered.

"No," John said.

"Alright. Well you just let us know," she said. Then she walked away.

While John was watching her walk away, another voice accosted him. It was a man's.

"Cigar?" the voice said.

Before John could even reply, the man stabbed two cigars wrapped in cellophane into his shirt pocket. "No charge," the man said. "It's your lucky night."

"No," John said, "That's alright." He took them out and tried to return them but the man was already on his way to the next stranger. He let them be.

John made his way over to a vacant slot machine and sat down to see if he could gather his wits about him. He was still a bit buzzed from the beers he'd had for breakfast and he could feel a sort of exhaustion descending upon him. He saw a window at the far corner of the room where people seemed to be going and coming away with betting chips. He debated whether he ought to get any chips, but could not decide what he would do with them if he had them. He did not know how to play games, how to gamble, how to win or lose anything. All his life he had never really risked anything, had never really wanted anything badly enough to risk anything for. He reached into his pocket and brought out his wallet to see how much money he had to lose, when he discovered Destiny's business card.

"Excuse me," John said, arriving before the exchange window.

"Cash or charge?" the woman said.

"What?" John said.

"Do you want to exchange cash or do you have a credit card?"

"No," said John. "I have a question. Do you know where this place is?" He held the card up against the glass so that it faced the woman. She looked at it and squinted.

"Never heard of it," she said. She made a face like she was disappointed with him and wanted him to leave.

"Okay," he said.

Back outside, the doormen gave him a hard time.

"Aw, leaving so soon?" one of them said. "Did you run out of money already?"

"Yes," John lied. "I'm spent. I have to go home now." Then he showed one of the men the card. "Do you know where this is?" he said.

The man laughed uproariously. "Oh, yes, my friend," said the doorman. "I know. Everybody knows. He is looking for Spiro's!" he announced. Everyone laughed. "Just get in the cab and tell them you want to go to Spiro's. Anyone will take you."

At Spiro's, John had to pay a fifteen-dollar cover just to get in the door. There was a long line which ran out into the parking-lot. John noticed that the line was filled with both men and women. He had never been to a gentleman's club, but he had assumed that it would be mostly men. He was surprised to see that there were women there also. Once he was in, he made his way to the bar and ordered a drink. It was very noisy. When the bar-tender brought him his drink, he shouted over the bar: "Is there someone who works here named Destiny?"

The bar-tender, who was bald, with bottle-cap glasses and several ear-piercings, shouted back, mysteriously: "All things in their time, my friend. We are all on our own journeys."

John wondered if maybe the man had misheard him when another man, whom John had been standing very close to said, "You looking for

Destiny? I just saw her. She's in the bathroom." He pointed across the room to where there was a sign for the restrooms.

John made his way across the room, trying hard not to look at the main stage where there were three women dancing on poles and several men sitting very close to them, passing up bills to put in what was left of their clothing. He stood outside of the bathrooms for a long time, waiting for a woman to exit. While he was waiting a man approached him and asked him: "Are you waiting for the John?"

"What?" John said. "I'm John," he said, and he instinctively put out his hand.

The man looked at him and then walked past him without shaking his hand, and entered the restroom. Just then a woman came out of the other door. John could tell she was a dancer from the way she was dressed. She was wearing a very suggestive shirt that looked like it might be easily removed. It was not Destiny.

"Excuse me," said John. "Is there anyone else in there?"

"No," the woman said.

"What?" John said. "Are you sure?"

"No," said the woman. "Why? Are you waiting for someone?"

"I'm looking for someone named Destiny."

"Really?" the woman said.

"Yes," said John. "Why? Do you know her?"

"Yes," she said. "That's me. I'm Destiny."

"What?" John said. "No you're not."

"Yes I am. See?" She flung her hair out of the way of her shoulder and showed him a tattoo there where the word was written in a flowing and elegant script.

John laughed. "Why would you have your own name tattooed on your shoulder?" John asked. "Afraid you'll forget it?"

"It's not my real name," the woman said. "It's just my stage name."

"Your stage name?" John said. "Are there other girls here who dance here under that name?"

"Not that I know of," the woman said. "Why? Who are you?"

"Me? I'm John. John Runner. I was supposed to meet someone here tonight named Destiny. See?" He held up the business card with the word printed on it. The woman took it from him.

"This is my card!" she said. "Who gave this to you?"

"You're not going to believe this, but we were supposed to get married. Nothing binding, you understand. It's just that I'm in a bit of a jam with my job right now and I need to have a marriage certificate or I can't advance."

"Seriously," she said. "Who gave you this?"

"Destiny did," said John. "At least, she told me

she was Destiny. Now I'm finding out that maybe she wasn't."

"Oh, man," the woman said. "That's nuts."

"Yeah."

"She said she was going to marry you?"

"That's right. Just to help me out of a jam. I'm flying back to Penn—ah, New Hampshire tomorrow morning. We were supposed to get married tonight and then that was going to be the last we saw of one another. It was all arranged."

"Wow. Well," she said. "I don't know who she was but she was pulling a fast one on you. Will you excuse me? I've got to go on in about three minutes."

"Say—" said John. He felt desperate, suddenly. "You wouldn't be available—I mean, after the show, would you?"

"To get married?" she said inquisitively. "No."

"What about for a thousand dollars? You would never have to see me again. You'd just have to come with me to sign the book so we can get the certificate. You don't even need to sign your real name. I'll take you in a cab and put you in one as soon as we're finished. You'll never have to see me again. I'll pay you up front, right here and now, in cash."

Destiny hesitated. Then she said, "I have to go on."

"Can I wait for you?" John asked.

"You do what you like," she said. "I'm not the boss of you."

She slipped along the wall until she was at the front of the room where she disappeared behind a fold in one of the curtains. Twenty minutes later her name was announced over the loudspeaker, and she came out, wearing even fewer clothes than she had had on before, and did a thrilling dance on one of the poles. At one point she shook it so hard that some plaster came loose from the ceiling and fell like snow upon the heads and backs of the whooping men in the front row. When her performance was finished, there was a long lull, and John waited for her to come out again. He continued to drink, looking at all of the various women who were walking back and forth from the bar to the stage, wondering if he would run into the one he had met on the airplane, the one who had called herself Destiny but hadn't been. He did not see her. After a while he began to wonder whether she had been real at all.

It was nearly 2 a.m. when John decided that she wasn't coming back—the real Destiny or the fake one. They were both gone. He decided that his plan was really quite stupid. In less than sixteen hours he would have to get back on the airplane and return to Pennsylvania with only a ring to lend his story any credibility—a ring which he needed not have ever left Pennsylvania to acquire. "At least I'll still have my story," he thought to himself—but John really had no idea what he could possibly tell Aida that would make her leave him. He wondered what he should do, whether he might find a woman here who was drunk enough to be persuaded to marry him. He looked around. The only people he saw were men. He thought about asking one of them to marry him, but he did not expect he would find that sort of man in a "gentleman's club." He left feeling very tired.

On the way back to the hotel, the cab-driver passed what looked like a small church that had neon lights in the front of it that read: DRIVE THRU OPEN and a life-size statue of Elvis Presley in the front of it. When he looked at it, a strange and bold thought occurred to John. "Pull over," he said. The driver slammed on the brakes.

"What is it?" the driver said.

"I'm getting out. What do I owe you?"

"Do you want me to wait?"

"No."

John entered the glass doors of the make-shift church. Before him was a small table; behind it sat a man dressed like a magician. He had a stove-pipe hat and a black cape and was wearing sunglasses whose frames were pink, the lenses of which had been cut out in the shapes of stars.

"Hi there," the man said. "Looking for someone?"

"I have a question," John said. His words felt strange coming out of his mouth, and he wondered if he seemed as drunk as he felt. "I need to get married."

"Well you've come to the right place," the man said. He produced a large book which he flopped over onto the table in front of John. "If you'll just sign our ledger for our records..."

John took the pen he was given and signed his name. As he was writing he noticed that each entry allowed space for two names to be entered. When he had finished signing, he was worried if there were not two names, he would be asked to leave. In a panic he wrote his birth-mother's maiden name— Jacquelyn Roads—in the space and returned the pen.

"Thank you," said the magician. "It'll still be a little while yet."

"But I have a question," John asserted.

"Well you're going to have to wait your turn, I'm afraid." The man pointed to a small lobby behind him where another couple was sitting. At a glance, they made John very afraid. As an individual he felt like he did not belong there, and would soon be asked to leave.

"How long's the wait?" John said.

"Shouldn't be too long," the man said. "There's a wedding going on right now. Should be over in about five...maybe ten minutes. Then there's another couple signed up ahead of you. Then there's you. Is your...partner here yet, sir?"

"That's my question," John said. He did not go on.

"What's that?"

"If I don't have anyone to get married to, can I still get married?"

The man seemed to consider this. "Well—hm. I don't know. Why would you want to do that?" the magician said, and he laughed, apparently thinking it was very funny.

"I don't know," John said. He mumbled something, then, the only audible word of which was "loneliness."

"Well—you'd be surprised," the magician said. "We get a lot of strange cookies in here. Last week a man came in said he wanted to marry his goldfish. There's no law against it in the state of Nevada. We had to look that one up. So we let him. I'll have to ask the Reverend...of course, it poses the question of what you'll want your certificate to say. But I suppose if—"

"Can I make something up?"

"Excuse me?" the magician said.

"Can I make up a person to marry?"

"Make up a person?" the magician said. This time he laughed very hard, and for a long time. When he had settled down he said, "No—I'm afraid you're not allowed to do that, sir. That would be fraud. I mean—I don't care, personally, but the state keeps a pretty close eye on us, and if they found out we were letting people marry whoever they wanted under the sun, people who don't actually exist—well, we'd be under lock and key faster than you could say—"

"Next!" Just then the doors of the sanctuary burst open and a man dressed as a reverend emerged, along with the sound of a recorded organ, playing a wedding-anthem. The reverend looked to be about forty-five, with large spectacles and greased hair, nearly parted on the side. John noticed that he had multiple piercings on both of his ears, as well as tattoos that seemed to cover his body, extending as far out from the sleeves of his frock as his knuckles. Behind him were a newly betrothed couple—a man with a long beard and a bandana who was dressed in leather from head to foot and a tall woman of middle-age in a red sequin dress and platform heels. A young woman dressed in white held the door and threw confetti as the couple made their exit. They were all smiles.

"Martini!" the Reverend said, addressing the magician. "Will you get this lovely couple their certificate and get them their receipts and on their way?"

"Yes, Father," the magician said. "If you'll just step right over here to this table," he said, rising from his chair and indicating with a white baton exactly where they should stand.

"Next!" the Reverend called again loudly into the waiting room. The couple in the waiting room got up and walked through the lobby and into the sanctuary. They were a quiet, unobtrusive pair. The only mentionable detail about either of them was that the woman had a large black patch over her right eye. After they had passed through the doors, the woman in the white dress produced a small vacuum cleaner and was busy at the task of cleaning up the confetti she had just thrown everywhere not thirty seconds before when the Reverend asked: "How many more of these do we have tonight, Martini?" His body was already turned towards the sanctuary doors.

"Just this next couple and then this gentleman," Martini said, gesturing vaguely in John's direction as he proceeded to look for the marriage certificates.

"That's it? Two more?" the Reverend paused to take a long look at John, as though he found something terribly strange about him. It'll be an early night, then. Cigars on me, then. Yes! Cigars all round!"

"Yes, father," Martini said. The reverend

disappeared inside the sanctuary and the woman in white pulled closed the doors. When silence had resumed, Martini said, "You'll have to pardon me just one moment. I'm fresh out of marriage certificates. I'll have to print some more. One moment."

Martini got up from behind the table and entered a door against the far wall. When he was gone, John looked at the newlyweds. At a glance, they did not seem right for each other. John thought the man was far too gruff-looking and the woman far too elegant. He didn't see how they could possibly get along. He expected the marriages that took place here did not last long. Probably most of the people were drunk when they agreed to participate in them.

"Congratulations," John said.

Neither of them looked at him. They both seemed inebriated, and were standing there, swaying in one another's arms.

"How long have you two been an item?" John said.

Again, neither of them said anything. They just kept smiling at one another, giggling from time to time. The man, John noticed, was touching the woman in what he would have called a sensitive area.

After a moment the magician came back. "Sorry about that. Got some more!" He held up a thin stack of papers. "Now—if you'll both just sign these, I'll have you on your way in no time."

While the newlyweds were hunched over their marriage-license, John encroached upon the table to get a better look at one of the copies of the document. He was disappointed to discover that there was nothing very elegant or official-looking about it. There was no flowery script or special seal; the signatures of the Reverend, whose name, apparently, was Dorfingle, as well as those of the witnesses, were pre-printed; the document was not even scripted on any kind of especially dense or encrypted paper. It was just a plain, old regular eight-and-a-half-by-eleven sheet of white office paper that said:

OFFICIAL CERTIFICATE OF MARRIAGE

This Document Hereby Certifies the Union of

_____ to_____
(full name of applicant)   (full name of applicant)

On This Day, the ___th of _____ _____
                    (day)   (month)   (year)

At The Sons of Ishmael Reformed Church
Las Vegas, Nevada

As Officiated by the Certified Reverend
William Jennings Bryan Dorfingle, the Second

Witness:
Ava Maria Dempse   Thomas Jefferson Clinton
John Henry Mercer   Mark Collins

He had imagined all along it would look very special and particular so that it would be difficult to forge. John Runner was no expert of marriage licenses, but this looked to be forged already. Despite the magician's claim that it would have been fallacious to invent a spouse for oneself, John could not help but wonder how many of the supposed "witnesses" listed were real people, especially considering the fact that there were not more than three people, other than himself and the betrothed couple, present. He felt he could have designed and printed a more believable looking marriage certificate on his own time.

Despite feeling incredibly disappointed with the way everything had turned out, and wanting to leave, John continued to stand there, as though awaiting his turn at marriage. He watched as Martini filled in the date on the certificate with his calligraphic handwriting, and then turned the document over to be signed by the husband and the wife. When it was all done, he gave the man a receipt and then rose from his chair. "And a wonderful married life to the both of you!" he exclaimed. He ran around the table and past the couple and held the door for them as they passed by him in a slow and ceremonious fashion, out into the quiet desert night. When they were out the door, Martini reached into his cape and flung yet another handful of white confetti over them. John watched it scatter quickly in the air and then slowly begin to flutter down, catching the light of the streetlamps overhanging the busy road as it did so, some of it falling upon the ground, some of it landing atop the heads and backs of the newlyweds, some of it catching the wind and traveling far, far away, out into the distant darkness, somewhere beyond the highway, somewhere John could not even imagine. For a moment, from where he was standing, if he hadn't known any better, John might have thought that it was snowing.

When the couple had gotten a sufficient distance away from the building, Martini returned in a lively fashion. He was grinning bigly, reentering the doors, as though his gladness for the couple were genuine rather than merely a formality that was put on for the benefit of his customers. He looked at John as if he had forgotten, momentarily, who he was.

"Now what was it you said you wanted?"

John opened his mouth but did not know what to say. He did not know what he wanted. He thought of Destiny. He reached into his shirt pocket and pulled out everything that was there: the two cards from the gambler and the lawyer and the two cigars he had been given at the casino. Then he remembered that Destiny had not been real.

"Oh, right—" the magician said. "You wanted to

marry…someone made-up. Well, let's see what we can do. They don't call me a magician for nothing."

"No," John said. "That's okay. Nevermind." He felt tired suddenly. He realized all he wanted to go back to his hotel room and sleep forever. "You got a trash can back there?" he asked.

"Yes," Martini said.

"Here you go," said John. He passed the two cards over the table to the magician. "Put these in there. And these—" he said, presenting the free cigars— "are for you and the Reverend. It'll be an earlier night tonight than you thought. Cigars on me."

He set them on the table and walked five and a half miles back to the hotel. When he got there he realized he was missing his hotel key-card, without which he could not get back into his room. He suspected that he may have passed them over to the magician with the business cards he had wanted thrown away. He sighed heavily. Exhaustedly, he stalked downstairs to the hotel lobby where he had hoped to find someone tending the desk. There was no one there. It was nearly five o'clock in the morning at this point. He noticed a sign pointing to a ballroom. He followed the arrows, entered the ballroom, which was large, dark, and empty, and found a couch that was not being used. He threw himself down upon it and slept until almost noon the next day when he was awakened by several police officers who informed him, before he had even had the chance to sit upright, much less remember that he had a plane to catch, that he was under arrest for murder.

VII

John had been an inmate at the Nevada State Federal Retention Center for nearly a month when he was informed one morning, just after breakfast, that he had a visitor.

"A visitor?" he said. "Who is it? Is it that lawyer?"

"Dunno," said the guard.

John had been lying on his back on his cot at the time—a favorite past-time of his now that he was in jail, awaiting trial. It was nearly ten o'clock in the morning.

"Well—do I have to go?" he asked.

"I guess not," the guard chuckled, looking a little surprised.

John seemed to be considering something very deeply. "Can you tell them to come back later?"

"Why don't you tell them yourself?" the guard said.

"Alright," John said. He rose from his cot looking very annoyed.

The guard inserted the key into the lock and made ready to open the gate.

"Wait," said John.

"What?" said the guard.

"Nevermind," he said. He sat down again and threw up his legs on his bed. "Tell them I'm busy."

"I'm not your messenger," the guard said. The gate was open now and the guard—who was very large—entered the cell and grabbed John under the arms and dragged him out of the bed so that his legs slammed into the concrete floor. "Now come on!"

"Alright, alright," he said. "Jesus."

They walked the long corridor, past several other detainment cells, until they arrived at the courtyard. There they had to wait for the door to be buzzed open. When it was, they proceeded outside into the bright morning air where there were several inmates wearing their bright orange uniforms, playing some sort of game. It was like basketball: there was a ball that was dribbled, and there seemed to be two teams, and it was played on a concrete court with boundaries. The only thing that was missing was the hoops. John had seen them playing this game before, but had been unable to deduce its point. What sense was there in dribbling a ball and having teams if there was no way to score? John watched them as they walked past. Someone made a pass which was intercepted and then everyone moved down to the other end of the court, where they continued to dribble and pass, dribble and pass, keeping the ball away from the other team, but driving it towards nothing.

The visiting center was on the opposite end of the recreation area. The prison guard who was escorting John was very fat and John had to walk slower than he normally would have in order not to outpace him. "Do you think it's my lawyer?" John said.

"What?" the guard said. "Who?" He was breathing heavily.

"The visitor," John said. He was only trying to make conversation.

The guard said nothing.

"How long have you been working here?" John said.

"That's none of your business," the guard said, huffing.

They walked on. When they arrived at the visitor's center, the guard pulled out his walkie-talkie and asked to be let in. They waited for a moment, then there was a sharp buzzing sound, which meant that the door was unlocked. John went in. The fat guard stayed outside until the door was closed, and then he walked away. Once inside, John was met by another guard who escorted him to the visiting room. The visiting room was divided by a transparent sound-proof partition through which the inmates and their visitors could see but not hear one another. The partition was subdivided into separate booths, whose walls were painted yellow and extended out as far as the backs of the chairs inside them, so that one could at least pretend there was something like privacy to share. In order to converse, both parties had to talk into a telephone receiver, and while the partition was sound-proof, the noise on both sides of the walls, merely from the inmates and visitors present, and talking at the same time, was cacophonous. John was expecting to see his lawyer again, a man with a sharp nose and a mustache whom the police had appointed for him, whom he had only spoken to once and who had told John, frankly, that he did not believe him when John had told him that he was innocent. He would have been disappointed to see his lawyer; but he was more disappointed to see that it was Aida.

She stood up in her chair when she saw him. He motioned for her to sit down. She immediately put her hand on the glass and mouthed the words "John! Are you okay? Are you okay?" He was glad he could not hear her voice.

He picked up the receiver.

"Hello?" he said. He pointed to Aida's telephone and motioned for her to pick it up. She did.

"John! Are you alright? My God, how have you been? Are you okay?"

"I'm fine," John said. "Just fine." He looked at her. He hated the way she looked. Her eyes were full of tears. "Aida," he said, softly. His voice sounded remorseful.

"John," she said.

"Aida," he said, turning away his eyes. "What are you doing here? Why'd you come out here?"

"I came for you, John. I came to see you. I've been thinking about you. I would have come sooner except I didn't know where you were. I didn't know anything. Everyone thought maybe…well, nobody knew anything. How come you didn't tell anybody you were coming out here? And why'd you do it, anyway? Do you know what they've been saying? Do you know what they've been telling me about you? They say that you…oh, John. It's just terrible. It's awful!"

John nodded. "It's not true, Aida," he said. "None of it's true." Then he thought something, and said, "Well…that's not true. Some of it *is* true, probably. Some of it." He remembered suddenly what his intentions had been in the beginning, and how irrelevant they seemed now. He had already gotten what he wanted. He remembered that he had only wanted to be free of her. He realized now that she was here, now that she had come all this way on his account, that she had failed, that she could not get any closer to him than this. From now on, as long as he was in jail, there would always be at least a partition between them.

"What did they tell you?" John said.

"They said you killed a woman. That you married her and killed her." Just saying it caused Aida to burst into tears.

"I didn't kill anybody," he said. He felt an uncontrollable urge suddenly to tell her the truth about everything. "It was all a big mix up. There was this magician..." he began, but stopped himself short.

"A magician?" Aida said.

John sighed. "What does it matter?" he said.

"It does matter. It does! What happened, John? I want to know."

John was silent. There seemed to be hundreds of possibilities running through his mind all at once.

"I know you didn't kill anybody," Aida said. "I know that."

"Oh you do? How do you know?" John said, becoming defensive. He felt a sharp pang of hatred rise in him for her at the prospect of having any single possibility pinned down. "How can you possibly know a thing like that?"

"Because I know you," Aida said. "I know—"

"You don't know me!" John said. "I been telling you that all along. You don't know anything about me! You're crazy, Aida. It's time you knew that."

Aida was silent a moment. Then she looked at him. "John," she said. "I know you didn't kill anybody. I know it just like you know it. I told them that. I'm on your side."

John looked at her through the hard plastic partition. He smiled.

"You're on my side?" he said.

"Yes," she said, confidently.

"Well—nobody cares," he said.

"I just can't understand how they think you could do something like that."

"Oh—it's all messed up," he said. He seemed to be thinking about something. Aida waited. John began to laugh.

"What's funny?" Aida said.

"You know, I only came out here to get away for a while."

"Away? Away from what?"

"Everything," John said. "Work...well, work, I guess. I wanted to get away."

"But why didn't you tell anyone?"

"I don't know," he said. "I guess I didn't want to feel like I had to come back."

"Didn't you want to come back?"

"No," John said.

"No?" Aida said.

John shook his head.

"But why not?"

"I got married, Aida. I was in love with another woman." He had meant to say it in the present tense—"I am"—but for some reason it came out in the past-tense. He felt like everything was in the past now, and he was alive on some frontier of the future for which there was no tense at all.

"That's what they told me," Aida said. "I don't care."

"I don't love you anymore," he said. "I never did. It's over between us. You should go home. I'm going to be in prison for a long time. Forever maybe." The way he said it, it sounded like a hope.

"John. You're not going to be in here long. The truth will come out, and then you'll be free. Don't worry. I'll get you a good lawyer. I'll get them to do their research. You'll be out in—"

"What do you know about it?" John said, angrily. He could not believe he was still losing this fight. "What do you know about what I did? Were you there? I got married, Aida. They took my ring off when I got in. They lost my certificate. I'm in love with someone else! Jesus Christ. What do I have to do? Confess?—Alright, if that's the way you want it. I did it. There. Do you want to see the body? Has my fingerprints all over it. It was in my hotel room so it must have been me!"

"But you didn't kill anyone. I know you didn't."

John hung up the phone and rose from his chair. He made a motion to the guard to be taken away early from the interview, his silent mouth explaining through the partition that he was finished. Aida stood up and pounded on the glass and screamed: "I love you, John! I love you! I'll wait for you!" When he was gone, Aida continued to sit in her seat on her side of the room and wept uncontrollably until she was escorted from the premises.

VII

Even when the Judge, who was called Dewsnap, came in to his own home and wiped his feet and lifted from his neck and shoulders the scarf his wife had knit him the previous winter, those present would rise to greet him. "Daddy!" a small child shrieked, leaping from the floor before the television, running to clasp herself around his legs.

Supper had long been on the table and was cold now, and Gladys Dewsnap was in her favorite chair with her glasses low on her nose, studying her stitches. She, too got up.

"Oh, don't get up, dear," said Dewsnap.

"Oh, it's alright. The stitch will still be dropped after dinner. Let's eat. How was it?"

"Have you been waiting?" the judge asked.

"Oh, not long. I've given Dora her meal, and she's all ready for bed—isn't she?"

"Oh please can't I stay up and hear about the trial?" the child begged. She was a precocious girl of about seven years and a half with long straight hair which looked well taken-care-of. She loved to hear about her father's daily work, especially when people's lives were at stake. It fascinated her more than anything she could have watched on television.

"Tomorrow," Gladys said. "It's late now."

"But mom—" the girl whined.

"Dora—" said the mother.

"I'm sorry I'm late," the judge said, looking apologetically at his wife.

"Kiss daddy goodnight," Gladys said.

"Goodnight, daddy," the girl uttered mechanically. He leaned over to let himself be kissed by his daughter, and then returned the gesture.

"Sweet dreams, my girl," he said.

She sighed, and trudged off to her room.

"So?" said Gladys. "How'd it go? Did he confess?"

"No," said the judge.

"You mean he stuck to that crazy story of his about flying out there to break off with his girlfriend?"

The judge nodded. "To the bitter end."

"What did he get?"

"Thirty-five years was the sentence—without bail and without parole. No deals."

"Ech," Gladys said, making a face. "It's disgusting that people who do things like that manage to ever escape with their lives. If it were up to me, a man wouldn't be allowed to touch a woman that way without getting his—"

"Gladys," the judge said.

"I mean it, Horace. They ought to castrate men like that. You know they ought to."

The judge looked at her with a pained expression. "That may be," he said, sounding uncertain.

"Hopefully he'll die in prison. How old was he?"

"In his thirties I think."

"I hate to think a man like that could get out and be given his rights back when our daughter...ech! It makes me sick, Horace—just sick to my stomach!"

"Alright, dear," said the judge. "Let's not let it spoil the evening. All in a day's work."

"Well—at least he didn't walk."

"No," he said. "He didn't." The judge had a distant look in his eyes which gave him the impression of being deeply preoccupied with something—but he did not speak of it. He picked at his food and drank several glasses of water and sat with Gladys at the table as she enjoyed a glass of port. Wine always made her conversational, and before too long she caught herself rambling about something one of the parents at the PTA meeting had said which had her all up-in-arms. "...Oh, but listen to me. I'm boring you to death, aren't I?"

Horace felt caught suddenly. "What?" he said. "Oh no. I was just thinking something."

"What?" Gladys asked. He could tell just from the way she was looking at him that she was not going to like it.

"Nothing," he said. "It's nothing. Are you going to knit?" he said.

"No," she said, turning her wrist to look at her watch. "I didn't realize it was so late. Thought I'd have more energy. I'm turning in."

"That makes two of us," he said.

He let Gladys turn off the lights and finish her glass while he climbed the stairs and made ready for bed. He had already turned on his side, had opened his bible and was pretending to read when she got into bed beside him and kissed him goodnight.

"Goodnight," she said. She turned off the light on her side of the bed and the room went dim. He looked at the bible, which he had opened to the book of Kings. A passage there had been underlined.

Give therefore thy servant an understanding heart to judge thy people, that I may discern between good and bad: for who is able to judge this thy so great a people?

And the speech pleased the Lord, that Solomon had asked this thing.

And God said unto him: Because thou has asked this thing, and hast not asked for thyself long life; neither hast asked riches for thyself, nor hast asked the life of thine enemies; but hast asked for thyself understanding to discern judgment; Behold! I have done according to thy words: lo, I have given thee a wise and an understanding heart; so that there was none like thee before thee, neither after thee shall any arise like unto thee. And I have also given thee that which thou hast not asked, both riches, and honor: so that there shall not be any among the kings like unto thee all thy days. And if thou wilt walk in my ways, to keep my statutes and my commandments, as thy father David did walk, then I will lengthen thy days.

And Solomon awoke; and, behold it was a dream.

The judge stopped there and only managed to shut his book and turn off his light before he dropped off into a deep, sound and restful sleep, knowing that yet another criminal had been brought to justice.

PETROPOLIS
Carla Prieto

The last time I ate a strawberry
it was like biting into the sun himself;
sitting cross-legged on your bed,
fruits, lips: sugar-coated.
The waning moon flashed a smile, crepuscular, and coy:
a presentiment of scything transfiguration.
We were infinite, then.
But not for long:
and hours later we're bellowing through each other,
asphyxiating in a cramped alley
where children throw fallen oranges.
We're having conversations with each other
in a crowded bar
in our heads:
like fleas slapped down by thunderous silence.

You should have been a sculptor, because
highest potential shapes stone; skin and soul,
humanizes marble; lapidifies the human;
And what remains when the sculptor and the lover are
    through, is a kore.
This, too, we have learned to call love.

I never reached the reasoning of the eternal voices.
But for now, I want to know:

What has become of Morning,
and what do you say To the Harbormaster?
How far from the coast was my one-man penteconter when
   it disappeared,
and how long until its fragments are recovered?
How many second-person singulars can fit a poem's verses
before you realize that
you are the center?

RESEARCH
Carla Prieto

Things have been coming together well,
lately my poetry has been
cathartic and I have even successfully resisted
the harrowing temptation
of typing "poetry prompts" into Google.

For research purposes,
I've typed "poetry prompts" into Google.
The results return suggestions as original as
the homeowner who hangs on the wall
an embroidery hoop with a red needlepoint stitched heart
    at its center,
circumscribed by the words "Home is Where the
        Is;" comfortable as an outstretched neighborly hand
offering a glass of sun-heated lemonade
on a scorching summer day.

I've a Reader whose eyes mine scan
as they skim over verses with feigned interest and
impassiveness ill-disguised,
fizzles of meaning gone flat
as bubbling liquid crammed into a space where pressure
    builds
but can't extrude because no one will drink
and nothing will be celebrated.
And this is how the reader quickly becomes appellative:

reining once-free words
becoming their master
by juxtaposing love with expectation, and naming her
Futility.
Several months ago I made it,
I know she Reads,
for the first time the contraposition
quite clear between that which words elude
and that for which we have created the word "fuck."
When he later asked for my hand
I said, "Which one?
I'm not ambidextrous."
For I was taken with a profligate poetess blond
a philosopher of O'Hara's flippancy,
and our shared feminist beliefs about body hair
being the propeller to jet her to me and away from me,
my own Marina Mikhailovna Raskova,
his ex-lover.

Reader itched her philtrum
and uncrossed her legs,
said she didn't know I felt that way
about her needlepoint or
about women,
this making her the true poet,
the one who rewrites the writer,
who hurls forward the phrase, as if pushed and
    toppled by a great wave from behind,
"It's non-autobiographical."

MÉLANGE
Carla Prieto

And here an invisible train's plangency peals the eyes away
from a mélange of ink and of pulp, of blood and of sweat,
   and maybe
some tears and some real heartfelt emotion if you're lucky.
The unlucky ones, yes, we're graced with looking up at three
   church steeples that jettison through a sylvan skyline,
dropped like gold ingots
on every other block. And by these standards,
the town's gentry is a pious one
whose salacious salvoes are protected by in-between
   alleyways
and blinds drawn.
Who are we to say anything about it?
You've turned a few carrots into roses yourself.
We all have, if we're speaking candidly,
tumbling and hurtling forward,
tongues loaded with silver bullets fired
as indiscriminately as a call-girl's compliments.
And in all our blind moseying and groping about,
we're fast to forget that it is in the dark we see best;
slow to remember that heard melodies are sweet—
yet those unheard are sweetest still.

FAITH
Carla Prieto

Here I am.
Thinking about you far more than I'd like to admit.
Now, sitting across from you on a white wrought-iron chair tucked
neatly under a white wrought-iron table that's rusting lovely.
It's like that for you and for me:
Everything always a little off-kilter,
toilet paper on the shoe;
an abdominal warrigal growl
announcing indigestion in the midst of the quiet contemplation,
one of the other.

But know this:
in me you have a home.
Come and go as you please—as you do—
and for you I will keep my foundation strong,
though I warn that this may shift and settle,
making my windows harder to open and my doors troublesome
to unlock,
as the hills beneath me flatten or round.
My hardiness, whose existence is questionable,
though in it I should like to believe,
remains to be seen,
as do the floods and fires, suburban burglaries and truths
disproven that will test it.
Until then, here I am.
Unequivocally faithful,

and with an electric hope that could generate power
  when a circuit breaks.
I beg you:
If there is a place away from me,
do not go.

My door,
like my poetry,
will remain to you always open.

LETTER FRAGMENT
Rupert Birkin

Out of my poetic/mythmaking needs, I long ago discerned what, if I had to find one thing, you taught me: the desire to be happy, the need to be happy, the fact that it's okay to want to be happy, that—in fact—that's all there is in the world, in the end. You've always struck me as this person who is almost indefatigably bent on finding and holding onto happiness. Not that you don't have other aims or considerations, not that your happiness is not often restrained, or questioned, or curtailed for the place of other people's happiness. I don't even want to call it a sort of selfish devotion to happiness, because that word has a terrible connotation, when the power I am trying to describe is so natural, so innate to you, inherent in your being, that it couldn't possibly be considered a bad thing or a flaw. Strangely, one of the images that came back to me recently was of the time, early senior year in Boston, when you impetuously decided to rip apart your bathroom. Your roommates were gone, and at some point you were suddenly overcome with the daunting thought that you couldn't turn back, that you would have to deal with the not-totally pleasant consequences of your action, but that you had been overtaken with the act, with the sudden desire to do it. And at some point—I don't remember if before or after—you took off all your clothes, and were standing there naked, amid the intentional ruins of your bathroom, having to work to get all of it—any of it—done, before your roommates came home. At least that is how you described it all in your letter, the way I imagined it after reading it, the way it has stayed with me in memory. The thing that stands out about that memory, to me, is how undaunted you were—you always seem to be—in trying to make happiness happen. You have this incredible power to try to make your happiness, to will it into existence, through the very acts and decisions of your life. You will rip apart a bathroom, after a sudden flash of the will, because of this desire to try to make things better, to bring them closer to that Happiness that you cannot help but want and seek all the time. That power—that power towards making your own happiness—is one that I all too much lack: I, who largely let life pass over me, who am more about finding happiness in life or letting it come to me through a change in vision, than in actively trying to create my happiness and bring it into existence, through the very acts and decisions, by altering the real-world fabric of life itself. You spoke the other night of just making decisions, and how important they are, especially to you: because decisions are the way you strive towards your happiness, the way you try to will it into existence, instead of merely sitting on your laurels like certain poetic/reflective temperaments who are too scared to make such rash and immediate decisions. (And all decisions are rash, when it comes time to make them: otherwise they would never move from the mind to the world, from thought to reality, at all.) But the thing about your incredible power, your undaunted devotion to happiness, is that it all too-dangerously skirts along the edge of holding onto one decision for happiness, even when—as will always, unfortunately, happen—it shows itself to be an insufficient happiness, only another step towards happiness, and not that final perfect Happiness itself. There is something to be said for my vague, indecisive, half-hearted investment in the acts and decisions—the reality—of my life: with that, my eyes are kept more firmly on the final goal, the ideal, and are less tied, less restrained, by the particulars, the real-world facts and facets of my life, which—no matter how wonderful they are—will never fully bear out the Happiness that, once upon a time, I had been taught to seek. Especially for you, there seems to be the dangerous possibility that, having made a decision, having chosen to act and now having to live with it, you'll end up holding on to this choice— this one attempt towards happiness—with too much fidelity and faithfulness, because you chose it, chose it in the past, because you yourself made it and now you must live with it. I can imagine—but this is something that never appeared in any letter—that, having finally finished your bathroom, days or weeks later, you had a moment of elation, when you looked at all that you had accomplished, and couldn't imagine anything better, anything more fulfilling, anything happier, than that very moment, looking at what you have just done. But—and correct me, my imagining, if it's wrong—that elated moment fell away, probably not immediately, perhaps not even for several weeks. I can easily imagine that, each morning, when you awoke and went to the bathroom, you looked at the tiles, at all the work you had done—perhaps even seeing the slightest speck of dirt, the slight signs of aging, and feeling, strangely, glad, maybe because your work has become something real, something that is lived with, that is part of life itself, getting dirty and fading and thereby alive, real— and were proud, seeing the evidence of your work. You may have even felt happy again, the same sort of happiness, though probably muted, that you had felt in that elated moment when you looked on your completed work, on this place—this space—of Happiness that you created for yourself. Yet, gradually, or all at once, it was no longer Happiness that you felt in looking at the bathroom: maybe you were having a bad day, or were suddenly stressed out by work or finals or something, and the bathroom—for the first time— didn't strike into you the note of Happiness that it had every time before. On the contrary, it may have even dejected you; in its own way, it may have made you feel even worse. But why was that? Why did that Happiness, tied to that place, that space, that perfect moment in time, suddenly lose its power, suddenly—abruptly—feel so different? E—, what I want to say to you in this letter, is simply this: don't give up the search. I rarely have it in me to try to make my happiness, to will it into the world, as you do—and, of course, so often at the expense of my own life, which I fail to live. But even if I waste— literally throw away—days, or weeks, or months, or even years, I am steadfastly, unconscionably, stubbornly, dedicated to the search for happiness, which I've learned to hold higher than the details, than the surfaces and the moments of our lives in which happiness appears. The one time in my life when I forgot that, was when I was in the heights of my love with A—. That was the one time I've ever thought I found HAPPINESS in my life, and wanted nothing but that HAPPINESS to continue on and on and on, forever, indefinitely, without end. But what happened? Things changed, I changed, she changed: HAPPINESS changed, faded. Because— I've learned through the lessons of many brutal years—that HAPPINESS is meant for moments, and not for long periods of time. Because HAPPINESS is the steadfastness to the search, to the aiming for HAPPINESS, and not to the forms that HAPPINESS takes, the ways it appears to us, along the way. That might sound horrible to say; and, like I said the other night, the failure to fully invest myself in my love of my girlfriend senior year at Vassar—the failure to ever love for FOREVER— meant that there was something lacking, something incomplete in my love for her. Like I was unable, unwilling to fully throw myself into the HAPPINESS that I had, that I could've had, in those few beautiful precious moments I had with her. But that is simply to say that my problem is, a failure to put myself fully into the moment, a failure to forget; yours, to me, seems to be the opposite. (What is poison for one, is the cure for another.) I need to learn to forget, in order to embrace the HAPPINESS that I can or could have in the deep moments of my life. I am too detached from the details, from the forms of HAPPINESS that life has chosen to bring to me. You, who make those details, who see their power in bringing HAPPINESS into existence, face the danger of holding too fast to those details, those forms of HAPPINESS, even after they've revealed themselves to be mortal, to be imperfect—to be alive, and hence to never be the full, total HAPPINESS which is the goal, and not one of these steps along the way. The one time in my life when I did learn to forget, it took me eleven months—probably more like fifteen, or even twenty-five—to learn that it was not the form of HAPPINESS, the particular form in which I found or made it, that was key: it was the dedication to that ideal of HAPPINESS itself. Do you know what Justin Vernon had to say about *For Emma, Forever Ago*? He said that, essentially, everything in his life spiraled to destruction, because he had forgotten to change, to grow, between the ages of 19 and 25. And it was only with *For Emma*, entering the space of Her, that he came back to life, to changing—and, to use my words now, put into his mouth—to seeking HAPPINESS, through forms and acts and decisions along the way, but not held back by those decisions, unable to move on. A— broke me—we both know that, or at least I tried to show that to you in the long, winding aftermath. She broke me (though I thank her for doing so) because I forgot to change, to keep fast to the Ideal, and to what HAPPINESS really is—what we really want—instead of the fleeting, imperfect forms in which it appears. On the other hand, I failed to love my later girlfriend fully—failed to love her forever—because I was too scared to fully invest myself in it all, to lose myself in the moment, in her, in love—to forget, like we have to do, like we WANT to do, when HAPPINESS infects us, overwhelms us, and fills our entire being. That's the choice of two forms of Hell, of course: we should want to try to split the difference, find the balance. And that's what this letter seeks to do, finally: to ask you whether you're giving enough weight, enough power, to that side of the equation that holds onto HAPPINESS, onto the ideal, and is willing to change, to grow, and to let go, to move on, if need be. I'm not saying that you should move on from Germany, or from all your life there—nor, for that matter, am I saying you should move on from Bethlehem, or from all that's here for you. What I want to say, is that, the other night, and even the first time I saw you for filming, you didn't seem that overwhelmed with HAPPINESS when you spoke of Germany. In the past, you were overwhelmed with it: in the past, I never questioned, I never thought to question, that Germany and everything there was a step towards your HAPPINESS, was an important and productive and necessary form that your HAPPINESS could and was taking. But, last Thursday, one of the first things I asked you was about Germany, and one of the first comments I made to you was about how you didn't seem as ENAMORED with Germany as you always had been in the past. That's understandable, of course:

you live there now, it's part of your reality, and it's not going to be the unquestioned, idealized, perfect world of DREAMS anymore. But...for me, when I was there, I never said I loved Morez; it was only after I left it that, suddenly, I found myself saying—involuntarily—that I had a wonderful time there, I wouldn't have changed it for anything. That's my own sort of problematic only-living-in-memories, only-happy-after-the-fact; but it's the converse of what your words at filming seemed to me to be. Yes, you were only back a day, and maybe you just hadn't gotten to that point of nostalgically—or with the proper distance—expressing just how wonderful life in Germany is. I don't know—I'm just talking, writing, and hoping it can help you answer some questions that you obviously are asking yourself, that you HAVE BEEN asking yourself. Because isn't that the key: you've been asking yourself, it seems, these same types of questions, even when you were in Germany. It's not a new thing, then, it's not just something that suddenly comes up in changing places, changing locations, changing continents. The other day, you said you were sick (or was it tired?) of thinking about love. I want to ask: how could anyone, anywhere, ever be sick of thinking about love, when love is the surest and truest, the most intimate, path to HAPPINESS that we have? How could you, E—, the one who implicitly, perhaps even wordlessly, taught me to seek HAPPINESS, be tired of thinking, of talking, about love? People change, they grow, and they grow old, more mature. Maybe you're just more mature than before, than the perpetually immature, perpetually naïve and idealistic, view of life that I have always espoused. Maybe it's only settling, if we look at it from the viewpoint of Idealistic naivete: maybe there's great power and maturity in being able to choose, and then to find—to make— happiness in whatever we decide. But maybe, just maybe, I want to ask, I want you to ask yourself: is that the only way there is to see? Is that the only way you want to see life, and to see happiness? Or do you not feel impelled, compelled, called, towards that HAPPINESS that knows no bounds, that will not stop with half-feelings, even with three-quarters feelings, even with nine-tenths or 99/100ths feelings: a HAPPINESS that will be foolish, and immature, and unrealistic, and impractical, yet BEAUTIFUL, nonetheless? Awhile ago, C— mentioned the three criteria that there are for apartments and for love: financial, aesthetic, and stability. Apparently you can only ever have two, and you have to choose to let one go. I, immediately, without hesitation or regret, said I would throw stability out the window. It's ironic, because I am the most stable person there is, in a way; and that's probably why I hold so fast to the search for HAPPINESS, at the expense of the stable sort of happiness that there is always to be found in any of the details and forms of the world. But that's the case for me; what is the case for you? I don't ask to know, but just because I want you to know, to think about it, to take my words however you will, trusting that they are probably truer—here, in writing—than I could ever really say in person.

DONNA DI FERRO
Anthony Delluva

1.

Her eyes peering through wet macadam, blinking away the rain that swells at her gutters. I follow her trail through the city that is also her body. The flashing neon of her synapses quicken as the endorphins from a bummed cigarette enter her mind—there are smashed cars in the intersection, traffic coagulating behind the blockage, horns blaring through the rain—what sort of emotional strife has she been through tonight? What sort of abuse have They put her through? —the traffic is yet waiting, waiting for a new channel to open up, an I.V. to be administered, a sign of some sort. I smell her in the rotten gutters that gurgle through the deluge. She smells of dumpsters wet with rain, stuffed full of fast food, coffee grounds, televisions, old socks, and guacamole. This rotten compilation of cultural refuse that is a part of her smell. She's been at the grindhouse, watching bodies bloom into clouds of red, flesh smashed against flesh—against this red mist, against death. She's crammed herself with candy and buttery popcorn, a big middle finger to her dedication to the gym. She is the victim and the cure of this pop cultural illness. The Asian district unloads spices into the smell of toxins rising from the macadam. She smells like this too, sweet and bitter. Her embrace felt in the narrowing of the street, the looming of skyscrapers. Thats what her embrace is like, metal and chrome sinews: full of a hardness she has acquired from never yielding willingly to the city. Her hardness is a comfort to us, a fleshy barrier full of black hair and elongated clavicles, a barrier to the avalanche of transiency that bombards us; cigarette butts hitting the pavement like arrows at Thermopylae. I see the wounds inflicted on her mirrored in the city. A shattered window, chunks of pavement coming loose in the rain, a drainage ditch overflowing with bile and refuse. Where is she? Even now I travel through her concrete arteries looking for her Umbilicus : that single lighted building that stands in perfect harmony with the rain, is not diminished or enhanced by it. Her voice in the collective murmur of the crowd— tires grinding on asphalt, rubber against pavement, metal against flesh, water boiling in a teapot—her scream coming into awareness. The smoothness of her legs felt in the deep blue windows of skyscrapers, and in the chrome of streamlined diners. Hands moving over chrome legs, cool and firm, polished by years of work and maintenance. Hands tracking over chrome legs, charting their form, the curve of substantial hamstrings, the narrowing of wide calves into piston ankles shaped by the unyielding hardness of the city. Her legs explicate the city. The city her legs.

2.

Her face frozen more stiffly than the Arcadian Styx. Her passions bent up in pipes, moulded into the texture of fabricated stucco. Her neck taught like the high-tension wires of a suspension bridge. Her dreams sealed into skeleton-frames by Sedaline torch. She fears she has become Monolith, a great unfeeling tower that glares out at the world. She sees the motions of passerby's, the pneumatic movement of arms from cigarette packet to mouth—does her face now mirror theirs? The chisel of the city sloughs off our soft and malleable flesh, making us in it's image. In our reflections we see the tactile sterility of modern buildings: the dullness, the monotony.

3.

My hands: seeking. My hands: ravenous, ill kept, desperate, worried, calamitous. My hands shivering around a cup of coffee. Something in the black ripples. My hands seeking ice-cold curves. My hands: clean and dainty. Her hands: dirty and calloused. Her hands closed into fists. Her hands ready to break bone. Her hands frozen like an icicle of chrome. My hands: inept, incapable, weak. Her hands: able, apt, strong. Our hands meeting like Ying and Yang. Our hands meeting like fire and iron. Our hands melted together into into a single mass: our circulatory systems combined, the ice in her veins, the warmth in mine. Our bodies: melting together in the blast furnace of the city that is also her body. Our bodies: a pool of hardening iron: out steps a discrete entity that rises above the city, surveys the good and the bad, and casts down seeds of re-growth and rejuvenation. Our hands, our bodies: liberation. Something in the black ripples. The coffee cup falling into the street, breaking open like a casket, buried woes spilling forth. Nobody notices this small transgression. Nobody notices our upturned arms and legs flailing in the dark. Nobody sees the pain as something discrete. The rain continues, somehow emboldened. The pulse of the city—ever steady—beats through the mains-hum of power lines, zigzags down streets.

4.

Her feet ragged like the surface of the asphalt. She stands on on broken glass and broken hearts. Toxic emotion batters steel-cut cheekbones, soaks into power-line hair. She is a tower stoically facing the chaos. She hardly shutters as Their cold looks cross her body like a wave from a passing taxi. She refuses to become weathered. Each night the window washing crew descends and wipes clean the glass of her eyes, so that she may see no more filth and despair. Each morning come the building inspectors as she mounts the treadmill , straps the leg weights, endures the dance classes. The inspectors go all through her infrastructure looking for torn ligaments and atrophied muscles—but what does she hide away? The deepest part of her withers even as her architecture is refurbished with stronger I-beams and new skin cells. With a single motion I collapse my umbrella and let her tears soak into my skin. They catch my hair, drip down my face, taste of timorous salt and years of being damned up in great water-towers.

5.

I know where she was born, I felt the tremors of the jackhammers that heralded her conception. I smelled the concrete that was mixed from the genes of her parents. I was there when they drew up the plans: blueprints depicting the construction of an angel, blueprints that were always being finalized, blueprints that left room for spontaneity and innovation, blueprints that carried the creative impulse. Even when her father lay fallow at his desk—overwhelmed by the possibilities of her—these possibilities blanketed his slumber gave off the light of stars, filled his dreams with hope. Even when her mother struggled with her birth, and the bulldozers and backhoes and cranes failed, spewing hydraulic fluid over her newborn chrome—even then a smile crept across her mother's dying face, for her mother knew that she was but a chrysalis that must be shed for the birth of an angel. How could the construction workers have known what they were creating as they put her together, atom by atom. Could they see that each individual particle of matter that they groped was forming a creation never before seen by the eyes of man? Did they understand that they were the collective hands of God? They—the disgruntled masses, the herniated workers: Brahman. Through beer faded eyes and coffee stained spectacles they saw her coming to life. How many sacrificed themselves for her creation? Yes, I was there for her birth, I stood admiring the promise of her freshly paved body, the elasticity of her newly circuited mind. She never knew it but the day that she stepped into the city was the moment of her birthday, the day she discovered that she had at last found a body for her wandering soul. I saw all this as I looked up from my coffee, and watched her step off of that bus that was also the womb of her mother. I never told her that I saw her on that day.

6.

Her legs like skyscrapers, she is rooted to the earth but on some days her head swells above the clouds. What she sees she cannot communicate to us—we who lay like grains of sand at her feet. The tempestuous breath that pours out of her mouth is but a light breeze by the time it reaches the city streets. Her decaying words obliterate on leather jackets, winter caps and headphones. I travel up an elevator shaft, step through the doorway of her mouth, down the steps of her tongue and into the cradle of her hands. They are cold and unfeeling.

7.

Her muscles like the bars of a jungle gym, she holds herself taught; torso and legs in torsion like a Michelangelo-image. It is this image that overwhelms me, draws me into it's perpetual strife. Her psyche in the sewers of the city, her tunnels lined with shadows, rats, chemicals, blackouts, diary entries and Them. A fountain in the park—fresh only to the eye—swims with her invisible meanings and emotions. We fall in love (erotically) with the city. Only later do we understand what this means. We forget that she is imperfect, we forget that we are imperfect. Only later do we find out what we have imbibed in our haste.

8.

Now I see her through a cracked lens. Each fracture contains a part of her: an eye, a hand, a toe. Now I see her as she was: a silent statue. Now I see her as she is: all of her possibilities converging into one reality—she lays on the street like a discarded bag of laundry. The city is but a symbol on an old map. It is already crumpled up, already discarded and forgotten. Will she be remembered? This woman of glass and metal. This woman of ice and heat. What will the future generations say of her? Will they look at the city and say here is the body of a giantess collapsed into her own grave. Now I see streets she walked still-resonant with life: her memory intermingled with the cafes, diners, and bars. Now I see buildings moldering to dust. And was it not written from the beginning? That the macadam would be her final resting place, her spilled blood a fitting epitaph. Was it not written in the strokes of window washers? Across her cool glass they drew ephemeral hieroglyphs with soap suds. They alone saw the wear and tear of her infrastructure, what she desperately tried to cover up. And was it not written from the beginning that she had to fall so that the city could go on living? I thought she was born the moment she set foot into the city but perhaps I was wrong, perhaps the city was born the moment she stepped into it. Her presence proved that the city was not yet taken over by the dead, and she had to die so that the city could keep on living.

[SURRENDER]
Cary Babcock

I adore slowly walking
in long, shallow puddles

when Spring teasingly comes
out in the exposed cold at the end

of Winter—it's like exchanging
words with someone you fear

you will never truly know.
I even find pleasure in puddles
you cannot see

the bottom to,
as they may be so profound
they swallow your ankles

in the wet sound
of an uncertain depth.
Yet, no matter how opaque

the puddle, it still reflects
and reminds me it is only

water that ripples, it is only
natural to dip beneath

the subtle swirling surface
of some satisfying soul.

[HAPP I NESS]
Cary Babcock

lurks as phantomfull, [she]   do
un   attached to docks on edge
of either of these states   untied

what if one Jersey and one Sylvian
pulled boats close together, wrapping rope
   through their holes to meet
where two rivers greet   ?

   what would terrifying rip tides
mean to lovers in/between
   prodding the water like their grey matter mines?

could the cool affliction send us all depiction
   of how rivers over-swellm   us and pretty
cities of hopefilled loves wean us

off the juicy glasses of buzz buzz
   sanctuary ? Clattering ringed fingers
   interlocking for the sake of the river,

because it floods and then
   there can be no thing.

["HIS OWN SMALL WIDGEON CRIES"]
Cary Babcock

a heart c locked with empty whys
as to the c limb we decide when walking
endless alleys of side,by,side

         above
one will feel people up   while
ot hers wink at the eyes of id ea

parting the c luster of people like weeds
congregating on the green feeling
of conversion,one,plus,one,equals why

in a state of stairwaying hopeless downs
a bar voice diamonized with time

ill-decided by thorough feverish
talk to get some poison out on top,without
knowing its purpose inside the mind/

    heat carries us away from the water's
    ways of feeding us(birds) nesting in
    and around our hearts. The bird far or near
    too complete to reap pear to under

stand its intent pointed with eyes of full
winged blue lies. Delicate are the bars
of our cage,

so I say, bendyourselffree.

Young and Old of Hugh Moore Park
Cary Babcock

Set on the island end of a teal bridge,
I documented gals, many dresses in breeze
colored summer warmth wrapped in green—
until youth pushed around an elder,
prisoner to a chair with wheels.

The way a man talks to a cripple,
from behind the head, with a tilt
of the tongue and a lean in neck-crane,
something must be said.

My eyes scrolled over them in curiosity and
they rolled a long while to the middle
of the bridge, where they stopped.

—Attention went back to my pen and page,
swallowing these consequences of young
and age, to the moment I heard young say,

in an angry way, "Come on, just do it!"

The sound beckoned me to look up
and find the old man weakly gripping

at the railing of the bridge, facing water
with trembling knees, pushing while
he pulled himself up further against rail.

    Frail and demented, I saw suicide
    being forced upon him by sturdy
    dirty words. No, don't do it, I thought.

The care-taking boy standing aback
continuously encouraging him.
    "You can do it!"
    "What are you waiting for?"

So I get to my feet with age on the edge
of death, peering into the plummet, and

he begins lifting his limp legs gingerly
shimmying himself one step at a time

towards the young man, now grinning,
supportively, "See, I knew you could do it."

So I settle back onto my concrete seat,
relieved and aghast.

Soon he bridges the gap between wheel
chair and young one, like a toddler
learning to run to his folks.

They propel once again, chair and careful boy,
only to return later and rest themselves
staring out to river, smiling and never knowing

just how much they frightened me so.

INTERVIEW: TERRY WOOTEN
Patrick Pfister

Sitting near the 45th Parallel on forested land in northern Michigan, the Stone Circle is a national treasure built and safeguarded by host poet Terry Wooten. For three decades Wooten has kept the oral tradition of poetry and the flame of art burning. Beginning each year near the summer solstice, Wooten hosts a gathering of poets and musicians who perform by a campfire to a background chorus of croaking frogs and howling coyotes. The atmosphere recalls ancient cultures that came together in family and community groups.

The following interview took place in the summer of 2013 in conjunction with the shooting of a documentary film honoring the Stone Circle, which was celebrating its 30th Anniversary, making it the longest running outdoor poetry gathering in the United States and probably the world. Dressed in his trademark leather vest and brown hat, Wooten sat on one of the stones in the inner ring and spoke slowly and easily.

Patrick Pfister: The Stone Circle recalls certain prehistoric monuments such as Avebury and Stonehenge in England.

Terry Wooten: I feel drawn to the plains of southern Great Britain…neolithic Britain. Maybe it's a cell memory or an atom memory. I like the fact that nobody really knows why those stone circles were built. At the same time, I know why I built mine. I built it to create awe and mystery. I built mine for poetry.

PP: How long did it take?

TW: Getting it somewhat in the shape it's in now, took four years. It's an arrangement of 88 boulders in three concentric circles with a fire in the center. It's an open forum for poets, storytellers and musicians. It's also a recipe for communication.

PP: Any special reason for choosing the number 88?

TW: In Pythagorean math—mystical math—it's the number of infinity, and it's also the number of keys on a piano. You've got to know when to stop. That's the secret of anything, whether it's creating a poem or a stone circle or a work of art—knowing when to stop. There's no better place to end something like the Stone Circle than in infinity.

PP: From the start did you envision the Stone Circle as being associated with poetry?

TW: I wanted to create a place where the words and the poets were the focus, a place where poets could gather in a natural setting that was very primitive. I also wanted to bring out the power of the land.

I think poetry has lost its roots. Poetry, ritual, dance and religion—they all come from the same roots. For thousands of years poetry was spoken around fires at night. It was used to teach people and inform them. All of our early history, myth and ethics were transmitted orally. Now poetry has become an academic thing and most of the everyday people have lost touch with it.

What I'm trying to do is bring poetry back home. There's an added power to poetry when it's recited rather than read. And the fire and boulders are an important element. They add mystery. It reminds people how to act in the presence of art. It puts the ritual back in it. Poetry, as I see it, is the ritual of life experience proclaimed in words that look and sound sometimes like prayers, or songs.

PP: During the actual construction of the Stone Circle—the week-to-week and month-to-month effort of lugging two and three-ton boulders across rugged terrain—what was going through your head?

TW: The dominant thought was, "I hope the tractor doesn't break." The diesel engine made a droning sound. The tractor would sometimes take many hours to bring one stone home and I usually brought them home backwards. I had a hard time steering because the front wheels would lift off the ground. There was a lot of concentration, almost like a loud meditative state.

The fifth stone I brought in weighed more than the tractor should have been carrying. I spent all day wrestling with it. When I finally got it set down into the circle a great doubt overwhelmed me, and I thought, "What the hell am I doing?" But in a sense it's the same doubt I've had, off and on, with poetry over the years, you know... "What am I doing?"

PP: Sitting in the Stone Circle at night under galaxies of stars, one is not only aware of the primitive, but of a tremendous sense of timelessness.

TW: Four billion year-old stones don't change very much. I think that's one of the powers of the Stone Circle. People feel it and it draws them back. It's always the same but different. The poetry is always different. The weather might be different. The fire might be a little bit different shape. But the stones don't change.

PP: As the night progresses and the darkness intensifies, the fire at the center of the circle becomes like a stage spotlight for the performing poets and musicians. Simultaneously, the dance of flames seems to conjure a hypnotic trance on the audience.

TW: Fire enhanced our consciousness. When we created—or were given—fire we suddenly had more time to work at night. Before that, you would close down at night. You'd huddle up. About three million years ago—a little before my time—it was almost like a psychedelic experience, or, rather, it *was* a psychedelic experience. It expanded consciousness. It expanded time. And with expanded consciousness and expanded time came expanded communication, which became language, which became craft, which became art. So fire isn't a simple thing. It's in our DNA. As Gary Snyder says, "Fire is an old story." You can't sit around a fire and not want to hear stories. We're wired that way. Fire and poetry grew up together.

PP: How did you become involved with the oral tradition of poetry?

TW: My mentor was a man named Max Ellison. He was sort of northern Michigan's unofficial poet laureate. I was really quite smitten by him when we met. Max taught me the magic of the oral tradition and changed the whole focus of my art from the written to the spoken. It was the last piece of my puzzle. He helped put together who I was as a poet because I had already pretty much rejected academia. Within a week I had started memorizing poems.

The knowledge of performing poetry, saying poems out loud, was almost like an epiphany or an awareness attack. But I wasn't very good at it at first because I had no formal training whatsoever. I was in two Christmas plays when I was kid. I was terribly miscast as a wise man and an angel, and I blew my lines as a wise man...I only had two. So I knew it was what I wanted to do but it took a couple of years to get good at it.

PP: You now have eight hours of poetry memorized. As well as your own work, you do everything from Chaucer to Whitman to Ezra Pound to Dr. Seuss, along with Michigan folklore, Old West cowboy poems and Chinese translations...in alphabetical order, sort of like a jukebox. How do you go about the process?

TW: Memorizing is just like painting a house. You do one board at a time. When you memorize poetry, you do one line at a time. I usually type up a poem, or I make a copy of it, depending on where I discover the poem. If it's my own, I handwrite it. Then I carry it around in my back pocket and I memorize one or two lines a day.

When I memorize one of my own poems, I almost end up rewriting it as I'm memorizing. I have a slight speech defect and there are certain words that I can't say together and so a lot of times that speech impediment will affect my writing process just a touch, since my poems are meant to be said out loud as well as read.

PP: When you're reciting a poem do you ever forget a line?

TW: Sure. Also, every now and then, there's a line of a poem that's so similar in rhythm that you might fall through it into another poem if you're not paying attention. So you invent little psychic wads of bubble gum and you patch those things so your attention, your concentration, doesn't fall from one poem into another. It's a lot of work. It's exhausting reciting poetry for two or three hours a day.

PP: The oral tradition goes back far beyond pen and paper.

TW: It's only been in the last 200 years that most people began to read and write. Before that the poetry that lived and was passed on had to be through the oral tradition. One thing about oral poetry is it's very hard to censure, to control.

PP: And poetry in general?

TW: Poetry speaks for a deeper self. It speaks for consciousness. Poetry is a song you say and it's not finished until you say it out loud.

PP: You've made the Stone Circle an open forum and, as a result, many other poets and musicians also perform there. That must sprinkle a great many spices into the stew.

TW: Trying to direct poets is like having a herd of buffalo. They don't direct very well. They're not actors and actresses. It's a different, a totally different thing.

PP: You could say the same about the coyotes. The other night they were making quite a racket.

TW: They're very curious animals. They sometimes come in and sit back in the shadows of the woods and then start barking at us. One night a young poet was sleeping among the stones and he woke up to find a mom coyote and her cubs nearby eating leftover popcorn. He put his head back down into his sleeping bag. It's fun to visit the stones in the winter and see the deer and racoon tracks going through the snow.

PP: What role does your wife Wendi play in the running of the Stone Circle?

TW: There wouldn't be a Stone Circle without Wendi. The stones come from her family's property. It's an extension of our marriage. She does all the paperwork behind Stone Circle, the stuff I don't know how to do and I'm not mentally suited to do.

PP: Does the Stone Circle ever appear in your dreams?

TW: Every now and then I dream that Wendi and I have moved someplace else, either back to our old house or to the southern part of the state, maybe back to Kalamazoo where I used to live, and it's always a really sad dream because I realize that I've left behind my Stone Circle.

PP: Can you imagine your life without the Stone Circle?

TW: I think that without the Stone Circle I would be a less recognizable poet, and Wendi and I would both be poorer people for the friends we wouldn't have made because of Stone Circle. If you come here any Saturday of the summer, you'll see that we are very lucky people in the friends that we have.

PP: Running the Stone Circle involves a great deal of physical work. Cutting and stacking wood, keeping the place manicured and mowed. Eventually the time will come, for one reason or another, when you'll have to leave it behind.

TW: I'm still pretty healthy right now, but if I don't find somebody within another ten years or so to help me with the physical labor, yeah, it'll probably just phase out. It'll be swallowed up by the woods, which wouldn't be such a bad thing.

PP: Looking back, how do you view the last thirty years?

TW: I was given a gift. A lot of people maybe wish they could build a Stone Circle but they don't have the opportunity. I married into a family with orchard tractors and land with big boulders sitting around it. I was given the opportunity and a gift and perhaps the vision to build the Stone Circle. It's been a lot of work running this place for thirty years but it's been a labor of love. As long as I can possibly do it, I'll run it to the best of my ability. The fire still burns inside me.

DEATHBOAT EXPO '87
Zak Bowen

Two men are on a lifeboat. In order to pass some time, one of them is going into detail about the history of maple syrup and its effect on the Canadian economy. The other, having gone a bit mad (and not a very big fan of maple syrup, either) stabs him in the throat with a fork from a ration kit. He then jumps out of the life boat, runs through the crowd at the nautical equipment trade show, and out the front door.

He later realizes that if he'd been thinking clearly, he would have just skipped the throat stabbing bit and went straight to the leaving bit. He chalks it up to hindsight being 20/20.

Even later still, he realizes that it had been a long time since he'd tried maple syrup, and that maybe he ought to give it another shot. It was a shame, too. He could have used the 75 bucks the life boat company was going to give him for sitting in that boat all day to buy some pancakes or something. There was that pesky hindsight again.

PRODUCE AND THE
MOVING PICTURES
Zak Bowen

"There aren't enough scenes in movies where people are eating fruit," said the produce manager to her young employee.

The quiet stare of the employee was misconstrued as a request for more input.

The manager continued, "I mean, they don't even have to be just standing there eating fruit. They can be eating fruit while they talk, or maybe while they're walking down the street."

"While who are walking down the street?" the employee asked.

"The characters...ANYBODY really. It's ridiculous, you know?"

Carefully placing some grapefruits on top of some other grapefruits, the employee nodded her head. "Yeah."

Mayakovsky as Surface Matter
Matthew Gasda

healing into shape
(go cast your body as a stone)
moving over the silence
like a dog on its haunches
to scare a bird;

tilting the samovar,
pouring the garden
foliage into the pewter
cup; heather-
flower, camomile
while you were
saying:

illness requires
so much fresh-air
instead of flowers;

so much
physical
haunting
pleasure
(so much
so)

RECORDS
Matthew Gasda

Did you forget the feline sun
Before it buried you in sleep?
We follow the structures of memory
Like music.

For a long time I've stayed here,
Outside the family romance
And outside of time.
Really, physically
Trying to
Endure.

OUTSIDE THE LINCOLN CENTER
Matthew Gasda

Moving to discover a way home.
Having fallen towards
The fountain lights.
So late arising, the cold
Tonight. And
Afterwards, there is the
Expectation of
Mountain flowers
And brackish rain.

But we've only concerned
Ourselves with lying
Lately. Aborted the secret
Of keeping afloat.
Erased our mouths again
At the smile

BOWL
Matthew Gasda

Water inside the grip of the
Earth. Let go of nothing
That does not heal.
Provocations are scattered
Across systems. What is
Inexpressible is what you
Forgive. The identity
Of touch. Ocean foam.
Indifference that does not
Yield. The late moon,
Curled back towards the
Center of the sky.
Acrobat. Dancer.
Like lines in a poem.

DISSERTATING WITH A HAMMER:
AN IDIOT'S GENERALIZATIONS ON
SCHOLARSHIP AND ACTIVISM
Daniel Nutters

I begin with two passages that will be the epigraphs
to my dissertation:

> *Few critics, I suppose, no matter what their*
> *political disposition, have ever been wholly blind*
> *to James's greatest gifts, or even to the grandiose*
> *moral intention of these gifts...but by liberal*
> *critics James is traditionally put the ultimate*
> *question: of what use, of what actual political*
> *use, are his gifts and their intention? Granted*
> *that James was devoted to an extraordinary*
> *moral perceptiveness, granted, too, that moral*
> *perceptiveness has something to do with politics*
> *and the social life; of what possible practical value*
> *in our world of impending disaster can James's*
> *work be? And James's style, his characters, his*
> *subjects, and even his own social origin and the*
> *manner of his personal life are adduced to show*
> *that his work cannot endure the question.*

> *The would-be specific literary intellectual who*
> *wants to work for social change will...have to*
> *fight off two demons of self-doubt: one from the*

orthodox left, who will tell him that his work is
bullshit and that real political work lies in the
organization of the workers; the other from the
ultra left who will tell him that he must connect
his work on traditional texts directly to the "real"
situation, our contemporary political situation,
or risk total apolitical rarefiction. My answer to
these demons is that genuine political work for the
Henry James scholar, as Henry James scholar,
becomes possible when contact is made with
the activity of James's writing, with all possible
emphasis on its act.

The first, by Lionel Trilling, appears in his famous
essay "Reality in America," while the second, by
Frank Lentricchia, comes from the opening chapter
of *Criticism and Social Change*. Both of these critics
are not just the tacit heroes of my dissertation, but
more importantly, they are writers that enabled
the development (if we can say as much) of my
intellectual identity; they, in other words, shape how
I understand literature, art, and its role in the world.
Lucky coincidence that they choose Henry James,
the overt hero of my dissertation, as their exemplary
artist isolated from the political and social world.

Beyond anecdote, there are several reasons why I
begin with these two quotes. In terms of "research"
(something I will come back to), my study of James

is also a study of romantic aesthetics—or the post-Hegelian romantic imagination more specifically—and their political and social relevance for both arcane literary scholarship and intellectual life more generally. Broadly speaking, to what use can we put Henry James, and the legacy he both inherits and transfigures, in our contemporary world? Another anecdote clarifies the importance of this question. I remember having a conversation with my grandfather a few years ago in which he (a child of the 1930s Popular Front) chastised me for not studying Dalton Trumbo, W.D. Howells, Jack London, and reading Alfred Kazin's *On Native Grounds*, a book he boasts about having quasi-plagiarized from in college. In Lentricchia's formulation, my grandfather is the orthodox left: "Who cares about aesthetics? Henry James is beautiful words about nothing," he memorably said.

My grandfather's position is not anomalous and I believe that much of the general public, if not our community of scholars, would agree with him. Hence the lack of "traditional single author studies" or traditional studies of any kind being written by graduate students let alone leading scholars in the field. Would anyone from my generation (the so-called millennials) dare write Geoffrey Hartman's *Wordsworth's Poetry* these days, a text celebrating its

50th anniversary? And if they did, how could justify an institution's financial backing? Anybody well versed in the Trilling, Lentricchia, or the other major critics of the twentieth century would think these questions absurd (as the humanities and their social significance is self-evident, especially to scholars working in the romantic tradition), but that does not stop J. Hillis Miller from beginning each book and essay he writes with the same refrain:

> *Can reading Adam Bede and Middlemarch today be at all justified, in this time of irreversible global climate change, worldwide financial meltdown, with a new financial bubble already building, and the bamboozling of the American electorate…by the media, advertising, the politicians, and hidden right-wing contributors into voting in ways exactly contrary to their interests? What use is "reading for our time"? The Republicans…[and so on and so forth]*

When such a sobering critic, one who exemplifies the act of critical reading more than any other, repeatedly questions the importance of his craft, maybe it's time to listen? Of course, I admit that while reading the essays, books, reviews, and interviews that begin in the same manner I detect, or least hope I detect, a hint of irony.

But there seems to be an additional demon of self-doubt that haunts academics. One tied to the bureaucratic hierarchies that govern how we train graduate students and propagate our "profession." I must preface these remarks by stating that I speak from my own personal experience, interacting with peers at two different departments in which I was a graduate student, and at various conferences and institutes in several different areas—"fields"—of literary studies. In other words, take all apparent generalizations with a grain of salt as I recognize, like William Blake's generalization, that "To Generalize is to be an Idiot. To Particularize is the Alone Distinction of Merit. General Knowledges are those Knowledges that Idiots possess."

That being said, considering all the external pressures on graduate students (the job market, money, family, etc.) there are internal pressures that ask literary interests to conform to scholarly decorum and that ask intellectual life to adopt academic conventions. For example, dissertations must contribute to a "field" already shaped by preordained debates. Can you write a dissertation or article that refuses to advance a field of study and chooses to read an author for, dare I say it, simple pleasure? Naturally, those who succeed in changing or shifting the debates become celebrities and gain the freedom to write what they wish, but such institutional success only sets the table for subsequent generations. How can we dissertate with a hammer, like Nietzsche, and destroy that table?

Nothing I am saying here, to my mind, is entirely new (though I know of no Foucauldian study of the deleterious effects of academic institutionalization). The students who I meet, and who I usually befriend, feel these pressures as well, while those whose work I generally dislike are ingrained in the ethos I am describing. In this regard, it shouldn't be surprising that, along with Trilling and Lentricchia, I gravitate toward critics who are not only acutely aware of this predicament, but who attempt (or attempted) to make it visible in order to engender change. The author of my first quote felt that societal transformation—the growth of the academic neoliberal order—was inevitable. The author of my second quote said to hell with it. But both of them were, like Paul Morel in Lawrence's *Sons and Lovers*, individuals who "[felt] the business world, with its regulated system of values, and its impersonality, and...dreaded it." Or at least their writing gives off that feeling.

As you might expect, Academic Fordism (does the metaphor work?) can be inimical to revolutionary impulses or activist desires. On the one hand, we have the example the opening essay to Barbara Johnson's

A World of Difference ("Nothing Fails Like Success")
in which she interrogates the institutionalization
of deconstruction: its transformation into an
-ism. On the other hand, we have Lentricchia's
"ultra left," those who tell the critic that he must
connect his study of Henry James to the real world
political situation. Let me provide you an example
of the latter by quoting Emory Elliot's presidential
address to the American Studies Association:

> *In May of 1970, I was a doctoral student in*
> *English at the University of Illinois preparing*
> *to write a dissertation on seventeenth century*
> *English literature. When the United States*
> *bombed Cambodia, and four students were*
> *killed by National Guard soldiers at Kent*
> *State, two hundred of us grad students gathered*
> *outside the English building in silent protest.*
> *In anger, one student called out: "How can*
> *we be studying literature at a time like this?"*
> *I thought that I could justify studying literature*
> *at such a time because I believe that literature*
> *teaches us about dimensions of society and of*
> *ourselves in ways that often penetrate more*
> *deeply into our consciousness and our lives than*
> *other vehicles of knowledge...But I had to ask*
> *myself why I was studying English literature*
> *when I did not understand my own country—a*
> *country that boasts about its values of freedom*

*and equality—while protests, demonstrations,
and urban uprisings were necessary for citizens
to gain basic rights of social justice and while
millions of its citizens were deeply opposed to
the government's foreign policies. My move to
American literature and American studies was
therefore in part a political move—though it
could not have been more personal.*

I sympathize with almost every word of Elliott's.
At the time of my writing, a week after the failure
to indict in Ferguson and the same outcome (which
was announced hours before I began typing)
in New York City regarding the death in Staten
Island, I hear many demons of self-doubt. Yet
writing is a catharsis. It is the critic's own creative
act, the "would-be specific literary intellectual['s]"
act, of coming into contact with, in the case of
my work, Henry James. Thus, I would ask Elliott
(whose work on the Puritans I deeply admire) why
he could not have leveraged his anger at the world
by reading Milton with the same fervor in which
Blake read him?

A different book by Frank Lentricchia, co-written
with Jody McAuliffe, called *Crimes of Art and Terror*
discusses the kind of politics we might find in a
Milton or a Blake:

The desire beneath many romantic literary visions is for a terrifying awakening that would undo the West's economic cultural order, whose origin was the Industrial Revolution and whose goal is global saturation, the obliteration of different. It is also the desire, of course, of what is called terrorism. Transgressive artistic desire— which wants to make art whose very originality constitutes a step across the beyond boundaries of the order in place—is desire not to violate within a regime of culture...but desire to stand somehow outside, so much the better to violate and subvert the regime itself.

All the significant literary theory (a generalization!) expresses this aim. I think of Foucault's and Derrida's indebtedness to Bataille and Blanchot; Trilling's diagnosis of modern literature's anti-establishment ethos; Lentricchia's reading of Wallace Stevens's gendered economic literary anxieties; Geoffrey Hartman's discussion of radical art; and Harold Bloom's theory of influence anxiety as "antithetical criticism" that could "open received texts to...the sufferings of history." Not to mention the important scholarship of someone like Johnson, who, as she admits, bites off the hand that feeds her by exposing the patriarchal tendencies in Bloom, Hartman, de Man, et al.

But where, I ask, is the legacy of that transgressive artistic desire in scholarship at, well, the MLA? We do "research." I am asked to define my "research agenda." If I was in England I would be a "research student," not a graduate student. What is my research? I read books and discuss books with others. I debate with a friend the political efficacy of Schlegel versus Kierkegaard. I throw my Herman Melville and John Keats into the face of his Whitman. I still have no idea what research is…am I supposed to find an archive? Well, at my institution we lack the financial resources of fellowships but even if we sat on a pot of money I would still prefer to read Melville than maritime archival material. Am I supposed to measure my scholarship in terms of progress? My dissertation emerges out of two epigraphes dated from the 1940s and 1980s. But maybe research implies book history? However I don't care where Billy-Budd came from, I am just happy I have it to read and teach and will thank whoever discovered it after Melville's death. What about biography? Melville was a deeply flawed human being, yes, but as Nietzsche says: "geniuses of [t]his sort seldom have the right to understand themselves." If the act that Lentricchia speaks of is something akin to Blakean vision, within the current and emergent academic clergy (those who came of age in the late 80s and 90s), where are the critics who do not recover some lost history of the past, unearth a previously repressed discourse, or diagnose and debunk ideology, but create and transfigure the world in which we live through the power of their own creative imagination? Does criticism feed off the object of its study, for life and sustenance, like Yeatsian bread crumbs, or is it parasitical in the sense that M. H. Abrams implied many years ago? These are generalizations by the barrel full. Maybe my reading is too limited since my refusal to specialize means I spread myself too thin amongst the various "fields" inhabiting the 19th century. Maybe I go to the wrong panels or read the wrong journals. Alas, a hammer is a dangerous tool when placed in the hands of an idiot!

A scholar who discusses these issues with admirable deftness is Mark Edmundson. Devouring his essay "When I Was Young at Yale" elicited much admiration and enthusiasm, but also a bit of sorrow and something like nostalgia for an era of which I came too late. For example, Edmundson writes of his first encounter with Foucault:

> *How many times did I stare with raw admiration at the picture of Michel Foucault on the back of my hardback edition of* Discipline and Punishment? *I gazed at the shaved dome, the tightened jaw, the (apparently) titanium glasses, and the eyes behind them that looked as though they could burn steel.*

When we read *Discipline and Punishment* today, there is no picture of its author. In fact, the book has been repackaged, along with all of his other works, in a new edition that depicts only a ruler. It doesn't feel revolutionary. It is almost forty years old. And what it resulted in, as we are all too aware, is *The Novel and the Police, Desire and Domestic Discourse, The Historicity of Romantic Discourse* and a library's worth of books that apply its genealogical method with ever diminishing returns. Do any of us feel the rush of excitement, the "raw admiration," when reading these classics of academic scholarship? Does the picture on the back of *Novel and the Police* "burn steel?" (In this regard I should make reference to the irony that oozes from the Lentricchia photograph on the back of *Criticism and Social Change*—as well his discussion of this irony in several *Critical Inquiry* articles). What are the sublime works of scholarship that we can't put down because they engender anxiety, dread, but also pleasure and hope? What works of scholarship, in other words, bring out emotions like our favorite poems and novels? Teaching Baldwin's *Go Tell It on the Mountain* moves me to tears. I read it alongside an essay called "James Baldwin's Exile" in Henry Sussman's *Idylls of the Wanderer* that beautifully illuminates the destructive force of Baldwin's hammer. A student of deconstruction at its finest, someone who resisted its institutionalization, Sussman's reading demonstrates a profound imaginative energy that further enlivens Baldwin. This is a rarity.

I've continually tried to read William Blake with any sort of coherence, yet despite my inability to penetrate the armature that is his symbolism I manage to take pleasure in my non-knowledge. I keep my *Complete Prose and Poetry* beside my bed, on top of twenty backed-up issues of *The Nation*, and read what I can. What attracts me to Blake and the romantic tradition, which I first came to through Melville and Baudelaire, is its anger, its rage, or its attempt to tame these feelings as it desires to raze (or raise?) the world. When I hear papers at conferences that try to make me aware of "climate consciousness" or the latent imperialism in, well, anything, I think to myself: I am aware of climate change, I am aware of imperialism, aren't you preaching to the choir? Scholarship that possesses an activist impulse seems merely to diagnose problems that any intellectual is already aware of…do I need to read E.M. Forester to have a better understanding that we are in the midst of an environmental crisis? Of course authors such as he represent environmental problems in interesting ways, but this seems to be a bit reductive, a bit like an opportunistic use of Forester. Research, I believe, leads to diagnosis. Criticism, I want to hypothesize (though I generalize!) is vision.

At the end of his beautifully written book *Why Teach?*, Edmundson attaches a chapter entitled "Under the Sign of Satan: Blake in the Corporate University." After essays discussing the troubles of higher education and his own personal beliefs about the purpose of reading, the liberal arts, and so forth, Edmundson inserts an essay that juxtaposes his meditations on teaching at U.Va. Inc. with a narrative of Blake's simultaneous need for institutional support and rebellion against it. We all know colleges and universities are in a troubling place, but by writing such playful criticism Edmundson enables us to ask the following question: to what extent can we channel Blake's creativity as we attempt to ameliorate our condition? How, his essay seems to suggest, does Blake respond to the circumstance that we find ourselves in now? This is what Lentricchia means when he discusses coming into contact with the act. Scholarship is a form of teaching, its pedagogy from scholar to scholar. When Edmundson teaches Blake, I assume based on his many essays on the subject, he asks his students to respond to the truth of his vision. When he writes about Blake, he asks us, scholars, the same.

LOVE SONG FOR A DEVIL
Carly Lane

Whisper me slack jawed
You maker of train wrecks
Whisper me death high
Whisper me ill

I'll be your painted girl
Bony-assed pony
Fuck a thick quarter horse
For your coarse porny show

Drunken and dandy
Tiptoeing the trainway
My sisters the sleepers
My brother the rail

I'm walking toward you
I'm lying down now
Whisper me bonfire
Ash on the snow

OPENINGS AND PROOFS
Carly Lane

Following the divorce I couldn't sleep in our bed. My bed. Friends offered couches and futons up and down the I-5 Corridor. I bought a car and a tent and a thirteen-dollar atlas. I didn't work that summer. The first summer I didn't work since fifth grade. When I didn't sleep with friends I slept in the tent. Mostly at campgrounds, sometimes in parks, a couple times on private property, having taken a wrong turn, too tired to go back, pulling over on the gravel shoulder, willing to do worse than I'd been taught.

Eventually I found a way into my bed again. There was a boy who baked me rye bread and showed me how to get back in. He left before teaching me how to eat at the table. I took to eating my meals in the garden. Wooden bowl in one hand, chopsticks in the other, I'd walk the tethered rows of raspberry stalks, pick my way through the thistle-down squash vines, survey the whole from the silver straw-covered potato humps, check on the strawberries, the tomatoes, the chard.

Sometimes when the garden looked more like work than reprieve, I'd walk up the street, turn west at the alley, follow the rock and clod furrows overgrown with morning-glory to the far side of the block, and from there cross into the abandoned orchard-cum-meadow the neighborhood association had fought to preserve.

Of the original orchard, only a few apple trees remained, crippled and crabbed on the high ground, the lower ones bogged and rotted, black stumps protruding at near regular intervals. Two surviving trees inclined toward one another on the farthest rise and one of these was especially good for climbing.

I learned how to a get a footing in the crotch of the lowest limbs and from there swing up to second-tier branches all without dropping my meal. I favored a long bough that stretched out exaggeratedly like a young dancer's arm, almost perfectly lateral and thick enough to straddle.

One evening, halfway through dinner and straddling the bough I heard a skittering noise close by. I started, looked around, waited. Nothing. Then there it was again—a hurried scratching. Balancing my bowl in an upper crook, I rose and walked the length of the limb. I was looking for snakes or possibly squirrels. It wasn't really a sound a snake or squirrel would make.

Several feet below, the grass was high. A hare maybe? A bedding deer? But there were no dry leaves, nothing that would rustle, and anyways the noise didn't come from that far down. Did nutria climb trees? I had seen them feeding in the slough nearby. Possum? Well that was more likely. As I made my way back along the strut of tree I heard it again, and this time so near my step faltered. I caught myself in a crouch, hands wrapped round the branch. The animal noises persisted: Whatever it was, it was inside the tree. Bugs? No. Mice? Maybe. I was up again and looking for the hole. Near my straddling spot, a bulging eye had formed around an old pruning scab, most of it was several times grown over, but a small opening showed at the head of one seam. I blew into it. Hollow. I drummed on the bough some. Skittering, scratching. My mind was a menagerie. I went hunting in the high boughs for a switch.

The first shoot I tried was too green to break cleanly and I left it dangling in the lofts from its wet tufted flesh. The second was soft, but came free with some twisting. I stripped it of its clustered leaves, peeled back the tines of its end. It had just enough give to make the bend from the eye. I fed it hole to hollow, turning it as I did so to feel the inner contours of the bough. My switch maybe two feet in, the racket started up again. I pressed my ear to the bark. One of them? A whole bunch of them? I couldn't tell. I prodded further. The scrabbling was frantic now and three times I felt something knock against my stick. Was that a bite? A batting paw? What was it? I stood over the eye, twisted the stick, made a jab. The tree went quiet. I was up against something plush, something fleshly. And just as I made to poke it inquiringly, the tree rang with a holy cry. The stick snapped from my hand. Unbalanced, bewildered I let it go just as that other seal of the Holy Spirit, a full-grown starling, black and greasy with an aubergine sheen, shot up in a dark flame from the eye of the tree, a wreck of wings in the leaves.

After that just the still and the apricot sky. I threw my bowl to the ground, pitched the switch after it, jumped down hard, but landed fine, kicked the bowl before picking it up again, walked home with my nails in my palms.

SONATA IN B-FLAT:
AN AUBADE FROM THE HIP
S.O.M

I. EXPOSITION

Any jerk who reads Wordsworth at a party deserves to be just as lonely as that stupid cloud.

Except clouds aren't lonely. If you see one cloud, you can be sure there's a whole mess of them pretty nearby. Just like when a honey bee flattens its wings to buzz its way into your pantry along the sill of the window you left sliiiiiightly open—

Late last summer. Except now…

it's Spring.

Bzzzzzzzzzzz—Once you hear that sound on the glass—

You know there's more where that came from.

Just like the Portland crowd on a Saturday afternoon. One 'ding' of a bicycle bell—and you better break out your latest flannel or run for your life. As if anyone in Portland runs. Can't escape the rain no matter how fast you go, which keeps us good and Vitamin D deprived and lonely up here (unlike the clouds, who have plenty of company) in the West by Northwest.

But I'm just kidding.

You know who was actually lonely? Not Wordsworth and not his limp excuse for a cloud.

Tchaikovsky.

Tchaikovsky was pretty damn lonely. Writing symphonies and ballets and concertos and just making stuff up like a maniac, proving that Form could be made into something as romantic as content. Writing with that stiff pen of his—as if he could be transported out of his terrifying sham of a marriage by having the courage to quit the drug—

all the trumpets and tragedy stuff that somehow still ends with a bang—

thinking he could be free and easy, certainly as free and easy as that chatty Wordsworthian cloud before the poet rubbed his smutty ennui all over it in his self-satisfied solitude of bliss—

My point is:

P. Tchaik was lonely in the real way. And it wasn't just a homosexual "malaise and martyrdom" twofor—he was composing a life—and almost got to the one he wanted.

Writing his way into a symphony that ended the same way that a life well-lived does—

Quietly.

And in the minor.

So you see—Tchaikovsky died a realist. Just like Beethoven died a romantic. Because—

"Everybody knows romance isn't real."©

II. Development

Jerks are real though. That guy is STILL reciting romantics in the corner.

Jerks jerk everybody around them in—turning all they can into copies of themselves:

Jerk 2.0s™ "All the Insecurity with None of the Sincerity."

So when I see the real (jerk) getting cozy with the not-real (romantic), I get nervous. It feels like that moment in a science fiction novel when you realize that someone is walking around the hero's part of the galaxy with a pocketful of antimatter—

One of the rare mixtures (outside of my Dad's cooking) where you know both sides are gonna end up worse for the wear.

Wordsworth and the Jerk.

Sounds like a Coen brothers' film. Or a Trask and Mitchell musical.

Or both. Ah...that's good.

Writing that down now so I remember to write the screenplay later...but that Wordsworth dude in the corner just keeps getting louder and louder so I don't even remember what...

Oh yes.

Wordsworth and the Jerk: A Musical (Dir. Joel and the other one Coen)

First scene is THAT guy, drunk on table wine and the sound of his own smug thoughts about poets that smugly sold daffodils wrought from the blood of the first generation of literate hearts bleeding and broken at the industrial loom—

Jerk 1.0 should be flattered by all this inspiration happening in his presence. Or maybe he should be flattened by the weight of his own ego. Or both.

Eyeroll. At myself.

I'm just jealous. Because I didn't realize that the Romantics are the new fringe. Wordsworth is inoffensive enough to get even the Episcopalian girls wet. I guessed wrong.

My delicate ego wanted to steal them with a smattering of Whitman (too sexy, too much touching and bodies and skin).

Or with readings from some Audre Lorde that I thought would convey my gender sensitivity when I picked it up at the local thrift shop (even though I really just love reading her alone while actually being gender sensitive, all by my-real-not-romantic self)

Or if it came down to social hierarchy —this one poet nobody knows (because the dude's poetry is terrible) whose poems I memorized on the monorail.

Just. For. This. Occasion.

Because it's not a party. It's an "evening engagement" or an "occasion" and OH MY FRICK are they seriously talking about the latest version of whatever Conan Doyle confection the BBC has cooked up this year?!

Right. 221B, Flat of Unrequited Homoerotic Desire.

That's another musical. An ironic, straight-to-off-off-off Broadway workshop production where the audience participates in the un-requiting of desire.

Oh wait.

That's what this is.

Wordsbro is the character that everybody in the audience hates (but wants to be).

And I'm the audience.

Oops.

#selfrealizationbomb #imdrunk #yolo

Unless, of course, I am Tchaikovsky. There are as many lives to Tchaikovsky as there are people who've heard Tchaikovsky. And isn't that romantic? #cliche

III. RECAPITULATION

Turns out—there's only one way to beat the jerk that you hate (and want to be).

This morning, when I threw a few glances at his naked pigeon-chest and poetry collection before I sneaked (snuck?) outside to call my girlfriend—I realized that only someone as insecure as I am would keep *Sein und Zeit* next to *Hosties Noires* with an empire of Austenite English to keep them apart.

Now that's what I call a piece of assemblage.

P. Tchaik would be proud.

That's a lie. P. Tchaik could care less.

Because he'd be busy doing real things like writing symphonies instead of drowning his insecurities in the saliva of a charismatic Wordsbro that remembers a few poems that the Jesuits drilled him with. Heh.

Should have known from his downward drifting gaze—

 that those Episcopalian girls would end up spending their Sunday eating brunch with their parents and talking about the garden, wondering why they felt such anger towards their Daddy all of a sudden.

I chuckle to myself, feeling grand as I stroll out of Wordsbro's apartment; thinking about those wonderfully sterile conversations that can only play over a soundtrack of sparkling crystal clinked against fine china.

"Klink!"

You know there's more (WASPs) where that came from.

Except they don't want to scurry under your window sill. They just want to watch you tear yourselves apart while they hoard all the honey. And kill the bees.

And then become best friends with your girlfriend as a way of trying to get your attention since, hell, might as well admit it—you're a Wordsbro, too.

To myself: "You really fucked yourself this time, yo."

Literarily speaking.

Because for how terrible Wordsbro is, now it feels a little lonely outside without his blather from the couch about "How nobody reads anymore"© while I eat breakfast, drowning out the words from the Morrison novel I've propped up against a stack of newspapers on the table—

hoping it doesn't keep getting bits of yolky sunshine smeared across its pages.

Smiling at all this ordinariness, I call my girlfriend to let her know I'm still hungry.

But she's too busy to meet me. So I just end up.

SALT THE EARTH
Melissa Monaghan

Whatever I have conquered,
this damp landscape of pines and
prisoners' sorrow, is self-effacing.
Salt the earth, I say; Let us
move on from here.

But there is still life here? Why—
Salt the earth; a hostile pasture
is dead sand. Damp, dying—
salt the suffering clay
and turn to leave before
the rain breaks.

BURIED MY HEART
Melissa Monaghan

by the red sands
was devoured near-whole:

I bet from even the parched mudscape
of a heart's safe-keeping,

you would not have believed
the blood moon, the burial it oversaw;

I, robed in the dark magic of loss, became silence,
I was the lilac queen
and fed my black heart to the ground

You would have always remembered
how the silence that shot through even the red heat
  played to our ears like lightening,

but then there was no rain.

Remembering
Melissa Monaghan

I frown—I signal growing irritation to my young lover
who does not yet understand the importance of schedules
(that the birds sing at eight am and the world leaves in dust
the lazy unambitious ill-organized)
or the urgency of time

His eyes flash with a familiar pain that looks quite like
love and his deep and genuine desire to make me happy
or at least satisfied,
the same pained apology from downcast eyes

as when he comes first or shows up an hour late
or forgets to pick up beer on the way over
and hopes urgently that his bright, authentic
face contains enough devotion to compel forgiveness

and recall from my cellar memory the naiveté
and hollow confidence of myself at nineteen, thinking
the world not yet ripe but sweetening itself for my far-off
arrival to pluck and devour its patient nutrients
so my face grows soft with reflection, and he places one
strong hand on the inside of my thigh—the other draws
    my cautious smile to
his eager lips that impart some lightness of his youth
to my lead-dense, serious, world-fearing soul

AGAINST CLOSE READING? ALLEN GROSSMAN'S "SPECULATIVE POETICS"
Daniel Nelson

"Against close reading"? What alternatives are there? Most obviously, there's Franco Moretti's "distant reading," which seeks to turn literature into quantitative data. And there's historicism, new and old, for which a work of literature calls attention less to itself than to the social and historical conditions in which it was made. But, less well known (and less professionally lucrative), there is also Allen Grossman's "speculative poetics," which treats poetry as invitation—a finished product, to be sure, but one that "requires an act, the completion of inference, acknowledgment."[1] Is this the act of a close reader?

Grossman, who died in 2014, will be remembered most of all for his poetry; but his 1992 book of poetry criticism, *Summa Lyrica*, promises to endure far longer than critical works tend to do. It is in this book that Grossman coins the term "speculative poetics," presumably to refer to the unorthodox method of criticism employed therein. Paradoxically, however, the term is to be found at once everywhere

---

1   Allen Grossman, *Summa Lyrica: A Primer of the Commonplaces* in *Speculative Poetics, in The Sighted Singer: Two Works on Poetry for Readers and Writers*, with Mark Halliday (Baltimore: Johns Hopkins University Press, 1992), 340. Hereafter cited parenthetically.

and nowhere in *Summa Lyrica*: it does not appear in the text proper, yet, as part of the book's subtitle, "A Primer of the Commonplaces in Speculative Poetics," it is printed at the top of every other page. The paradox is one that Grossman knew intimately: poems, he reminds us often, declare absence and deny absence in a single movement.

Speculative poetics is never defined, then; its stance toward close reading, whether hostile or friendly, is not declared. But in a brief "Introductory Note" to *Summa Lyrica*, Grossman gestures toward a definition of his method. "My purpose," he writes, "is to bring to mind 'the poem,' as an object of thought and as an instrument for thinking...I intend to facilitate (and exemplify) thinking as it may arise in the course of inquiry directed toward the meaning of poetic structures" (207, emphasis in original). Through this special mode of "facilitat[ing] (and exemplify[ing]) thinking," Grossman attempts in *Summa Lyrica* a rare feat: to define the nature and purpose of poetry, "the poem," without describing or analyzing individual poems. In this essay I adopt a similarly speculative approach: instead of discussing Grossman's ideas in detail, I address some theoretical questions that his book's unusual method raises about the practice of poetry criticism. In brief, my aim is to put Grossman's alternative to close reading—if that is indeed what it is—to the test.

In order to provide a base understanding of Grossman's method, I will begin by quoting four representative statements from *Summa Lyrica*, which I refer to, explicitly and implicitly, throughout the essay. Although these quotations will seem exceptional because of their almost prophetic tone, this mode of speaking about poetry is not an exception to the rule of Grossman's writing style. Aphorisms such as the following, interspersed with elaborating comments, quotations, and reflections, make up the bulk of *Summa Lyrica*'s one hundred and eighty pages. "The function of poetry is to obtain for everybody one kind of success at the limits of the autonomy of the will" (209). "Wherever the philosopher says per impossible the poet shows the way" (247). "The value of the poem for the reader of the poem flows from the acknowledgment which it enforces that something not the self is" (250). "In poetry language has gone strange. The strangeness in poetic language arises from the presence of the eidos, the presence of presence. An exceptional act of consciousness is required to greet this presence" (232).

As I said, this essay is primarily concerned not with the meaning of these or other of Grossman's aphorisms, but with a question about method: do pronouncements such as these qualify as literary criticism? In argument as well as style, however, each of the sentences I've quoted pertains to the essay's central subject: the relation between, on one hand, the poet's departures from cognitive and linguistic norms, and on the other hand, the critic's departures from disciplinary norms—those of literary criticism in particular and of expository writing in general. Taking *Summa Lyrica* as exemplary of a criticism whose primary mode is speculation rather than argument or analysis, I will ask whether the speculative critic's departures from evidence-based reasoning are warranted by poetry's disregard for what Emily Dickinson called "this timid life of Evidence." To put the question in Grossman's terms, are critics wrong to join poets in their efforts to "show the way" "wherever the philosopher says per impossible"? Or is the critic's task, like the poet's task, to defy the limits and norms that restrict "the autonomy of the will"? Is "autonomy of the will" something that we want poetry critics to aspire to?

So far I have framed this question as an inquiry about the extent of the critic's freedom; but the same question can be approached from a less abstract, more practical perspective. Are the methods of close reading and expository writing invariably useful when one's subject is poetry? If the experience of reading a poem is, as Grossman insists, in large part an intuitive, non-rational experience, doesn't the critic neglect a crucial aspect of that experience by focusing on what can be deduced from the words on the page? "In poetry," Grossman writes, "language has gone strange" (232). This conception of poetic language as not just strange but going strange, erring from normalcy, indicates the rationale behind speculative criticism's departures from protocol, and indeed from poems as they exist on the page. For Grossman, there is something counterintuitive about interpreters' efforts to rein in poetic language and bring it within the bounds of accountable speech—speech, I mean, that is capable both of explaining and of being explained. Since the poet's wish (to quote Dickinson again) is to "range Boundlessness," the speculative critic tries to join her in that unmapped space, rather than draw up an account of her exploits.

It's not an accident that the language of accounting and accountability crops up in this discussion. Interpretation of poetry is often—perhaps too often—a kind of reckoning. The critic reckons in two senses: she reckons with a poem by trying to make sense of it; and she reckons its value by counting up what we gain by it—as well as what we lose. Yet one of the "commonplaces in speculative poetics" alluded to in *Summa Lyrica*'s subtitle is that the logic of poetry is incommensurable with ordinary logic, and that consequently the value of a poem—what we learn or gain from it—cannot be measured by ordinary standards of value. Instead of reckoning, therefore, the critic of Grossman's type speculates, again in two senses: she posits ideas and theories that aren't based on direct evidence; and she is invested in discovering sources of value which, being indigenous to poetry, are obscure and insubstantial.

Thus we can identify two opposed tendencies in poetry criticism: on the one hand, the "reckoning" critic's meticulous attention to the evidence before her eyes; on the other hand, the speculative critic's commitment to the intuitive and unverifiable. Antithetical as these tendencies appear, however, I hope to make a case for speculative criticism by showing that the rationale behind it is based on the same premises that underlie more accepted interpretive methods.

Two things are helpful to keep in mind as we look for common ground between traditional or "reckoning" criticism and speculative poetics. First, my earlier suggestion, that the attempt to "rein in" and rationalize poetic language is counterintuitive, is not as romantic as it might seem, nor does wariness of rational explanation necessarily mark speculative poetics as mystical or esoteric. For there is an influential school of critical thought, of which Harold Bloom's theory of "strong misreading" is the most famous example, which holds that the truest response to a poem is simply another poem, and that the truest interpretation is likewise one that echoes the estranged speech and errant logic of poetry, in addition to organizing and explaining it.[2] This line of thinking provides rational support, as well, for the speculative critic's assumption that poetic value cannot be measured. If, as Bloom has argued, poetic "strength" is a function of poetic influence, then a poem's value lies not in its language per se but in the countless obscure ways in which its language echoes, responds to, "misreads," and even exorcises the language and tropes of earlier poems. Poetic value cannot be located within the specific words, tropes, and formal properties of individual poems, because poetry is as much a phenomenon of shared speech and shared conventions as it is a phenomenon of departure from the common. As Grossman puts it, "in lyric the story of a singular occasion of speaking is inscribed upon the history of all speaking" (233).

---

2 A similar line of thinking can be found in *Real Presences* (Chicago: University of Chicago Press, 1991), in which George Steiner argues that the finest criticism of art is to be found in art itself: "structure is itself interpretation and composition is criticism" (21). Charles Bernstein's theory of "creative wreading," which posits writing as a mode of creative, active reading, is a more recent case in point. See "Creative Wreading & Aesthetic Judgment" and "Wreading, Writing, Wresponding" in Bernstein's *Attack of the Difficult Poems* (Chicago: University of Chicago Press, 2011).

The second thing to keep in mind when considering the relation between the two critical approaches I've described is simply the subtitle of *Summa Lyrica*, which yokes the practice of "speculative poetics" with the seemingly antipathetic notion of "commonplaces." A book that calls itself "A Primer of the Commonplaces in Speculative Poetics" evidently intends its speculations to be grounded in, and to make departures from, places we are all familiar with. Even its primary title, *Summa Lyrica*, suggests that while the author's method is unorthodox, his subjects are rudimentary. According to Eileen Sweeney, when medieval philosophers adopted the summa form their purpose was "twofold: first, to completely emancipate the subject matter...from the structure dictated either by scripture or authoritative sources; and second, to cover completely an entire discipline, often but not always, in summary form."[3] However unpredictably Grossman's book departs from protocol, then, its points of departure are in a fine sense radical, not exotic or esoteric: they are the root ideas and tropes upon which both the writing and the interpretation of poetry are premised.

The two concepts of poetic influence and poetic commonplaces provide a basis for understanding why

---

3   "Literary Forms of Medieval Philosophy," in *The Stanford Encyclopedia of Philosophy* (Summer 2013 Edition), ed. Edward N. Zalta.

a critic like Grossman, when he tries to reckon with the evidence of poetry, feels the need to supplement, and at times to supplant, textual analysis with aesthetic and philosophical speculation. The evidence of a poem consists not just of its own, individual characteristics, but also of the characteristics and conditions that it shares with all poems. Hence the abstract, generalizing bent of Grossman's summa: the main question it asks is not, how do individual poems address their subject matter?, but instead, what do poetic modes of address in general imply about the lyric speaker's relation to the world, and about speech situations as a whole? The book is particularly concerned with the set of age-old conventions that define the parameters of the poet's speech: the lyric "I," the absence of the beloved, the blank space between lines and stanzas, even the "silence" out of which poems emerge and into which they return. While Grossman's preoccupation with these matters might suggest an indifference to the critic's customary task of describing, explaining, and interpreting, his goal is in fact to develop more thoroughgoing explanations for the exceptional nature of poetic utterance.

The foregoing will suffice, I hope, to account for Grossman's departures from the critic's ordinary practice of close reading. What remains to be accounted for are his more egregious departures from the stylistic norms of discursive reasoning and expository writing. The question, as I phrased it toward the start of this essay, is whether departures of this kind are warranted by poets' own deviations from cogency. Judging by *Summa Lyrica* alone, it is evident that poetry critics today are at least in some circumstances permitted to speak with the authority of inspiration, rather than the authority of the expert reasoner or the meticulous analyst. But unless we inquire into the rationale for granting such permission, we'll have no way of distinguishing between productive critical departures and aimless effusions. So in the remainder of the essay, I will try to test the basis of the inspired critic's authority, by engaging in some speculations of my own on the subject of poetic inspiration.

If we look back at the four quotations with which I began, we'll find that the kind of inspiration *Summa Lyrica* is concerned with is as much a phenomenon of reading and interpretation as it is a phenomenon of writing. Inspired language as Grossman defines it is "language [that] has gone strange": language that has encountered and been breathed into by what he calls simply "something not the self." And this encounter with otherness is as much the reader's as it is the poet's: "The value of the poem for the reader of the poem flows from the acknowledgment which it enforces that something not the self is." Defined in this way, inspiration is not an experience reserved for poets. The poem's capacity to estrange and inspire does not "flow" from that mysterious something to which poets have special access; it flows from the language that enables the poet, and forces the reader, to acknowledge that thing's existence. This is not to retract my earlier, Harold Bloomian observation that a poem consists of shared, echoed language as well as of its own measured and measurable words. Rather, the point is that echoing is poetry's primary means of representation. Whether the poet's inspiring, estranging encounter was with a precursor's language or with an actual person or thing, that encounter is only preserved in the form of tonal and linguistic reverberations. The original source of inspiration cannot be accessed directly, by reader or by poet.

From these observations we can conclude that poetic inspiration is both obscure and unusually communicable. One of the commonplace paradoxes explored in *Summa Lyrica* is that the reader of a poem has a strong sense of the inspiring object's presence, despite its obvious absence. The critic may have no knowledge of, let alone direct contact with, the source of the poet's inspiration. Yet if she is alert to the otherness of the poet's language—if she yields to the acknowledgement it enforces, "that something not the self is"—she may feel compelled not just to describe that otherness but to "acknowledge" and "greet" it with a strangeness of her own discovering. The philosopher Gaston Bachelard describes the encounter in this way: "The poet does not confer the past of his image upon me, and yet his image immediately takes root in me."[4] So, inspiration as a kind of grafting or transplanting, not of the poet's past, but of a dynamic, living "image"—a term that usefully combines the linguistic with the experiential.

The critic's impulse to "greet" the otherness of inspired speech derives from what Grossman calls the "eidetic function" of poetry: its capacity to convince both reader and speaker that something is present which is obviously absent. "The strangeness in poetic language," he writes, "arises from the presence of the eidos, the presence of presence. An exceptional act of consciousness is required to greet this presence." And in an important parenthesis, he clarifies what he means, and doesn't mean, by "the eidos": "(The Greek word eidos is here used in its Homeric sense as the form or beauty of the person...No implication of the Platonic-Husserlian sense [idea or essence] is here intended except insofar as the sustaining and ideal image of man is the countenance or shape of the person, the basis of human recognition)" (232-33, brackets in original).

4 *The Poetics of Space*, trans. Maria Jolas (New York: Orion Press, 1964), xiii.

This is a typically difficult passage, but I think the crux of it is none other than the paradox of inspiration that we've been considering. A poem is an exercise in mediation, yet its value lies not in the substantial presence that it pretends to mediate, but in the very act of mediation—of presenting or echoing presence. "The strangeness in poetic language arises from the presence of the eidos, the presence of presence," Grossman says. Poetic language is strange because it asserts presence in the face of undeniable absence—or rather, it's strange because, despite the absurdity of this assertion, it evinces in the speaker, and evokes in the reader, a powerful sense of conviction. (As a more recent article by Grossman puts it, "poetry is the most valuable thing we have, but radically untrue.")[5] This paradox explains Grossman's insistence that the eidos is not a phenomenon of inner truth or "essence." On the contrary, it hinges upon a play of surfaces: what matters is not substance but "form or beauty." In particular, "the sustaining and ideal image of man" that poetry conveys is comprised not of a person's interiority (which is necessarily unavailable to the reader, and even to the poet) but of what Grossman calls "the countenance or shape of the person." A person's shape—the way in which she or he at once conforms to and departs from the generic shape of

---

5 "On Communicative Difficulty in General and 'Difficult' Poetry in Particular: The Example of Hart Crane's 'The Broken Tower,'" *Chicago Review* 53.2/3 (2007): 141.

the human—is "the basis of human recognition." So it is with a poem, which must depart and conform at the same time: achieve singularity while building on common ground.

What special kind of verbal artistry is it that can present the "sustaining and ideal image of man" without digressing into descriptions of a particular man's interiority? How do poets make their language depart from the normative and common in such a way that the words return to us bearing more ideal, more sustaining, and more authentically common images?

Perhaps these are questions that only poems, not their interpreters, can answer. How can an interpreter convey what this exceptional language is and does without simply putting the poems before us? I hope to have shown in this essay that Allen Grossman's book offers a powerful answer to this last question. It exemplifies a mode of criticism that acknowledges the linguistic exceptionalism of poetry not by way of description, but by way of greeting. "An exceptional act of consciousness is required to greet this presence." The speculative critic meets the poem halfway; she goes out and greets it, not with a poem of her own, but with the "exceptional act of consciousness" that the poem has demanded of her. "Reading requires an act," Grossman insists: "the completion of inference, acknowledgment." The speculative critic makes a record of this act in order to record, in turn, the exceptionalism of the poet's own cognitive and linguistic feats. Meeting the poem halfway, she measures both how far the poet has departed from the common, and how remote is the common ground between poet and reader.

But the question remains: is this the act of a close reader? It depends, I want to say, on what the outgoing reader hopes to get close to: a discrete linguistic entity, or the always receding source of a poem's echoing. More precisely, it depends on how the speculative critic perceives herself vis-à-vis the poet: as an ambassador, mediating between poet and public, or as a rival inventor. Harold Bloom and his colleagues accustomed an earlier generation to think of critics as poets' rivals in imaginative power and formal acumen—as if critics suffered from an "anxiety" of their own, not of influence but of subordination. In recent decades this habit of thinking has become foreign to us again—a trend to which Allen Grossman would appear to stand in opposition. Yet *Summa Lyrica* offers a model of criticism that feels like a middle way. Aspiring but not anxious, admiring but not deferential, the speculative critic is a sort of errant ambassador, with private agendas as well as public ones. It seems unlikely, but perhaps in future years a criticism of greeting and acknowledging—close reading that looks into the distance—will become as firmly established as the formalisms and historicisms practiced by today's close and distant readers.

BIBLIOGRAPHY

Bachelard, Gaston. *The Poetics of Space*. Translated by Maria Jolas. New York: Orion, 1964.

Bernstein, Charles. *Attack of the Difficult Poems: Essays and Inventions*. Chicago: University of Chicago Press, 2011.

Grossman, Allen. *Summa Lyrica: A Primer of the Commonplaces in Speculative Poetics*. In *The Sighted Singer: Two Works on Poetry for Readers and Writers*, 205-384, with Mark Halliday. Baltimore: Johns Hopkins University Press, 1992.

Grossman, Allen. "On Communicative Difficulty in General and 'Difficult' Poetry in Particular: The Example of Hart Crane's 'The Broken Tower.'" *Chicago Review* 53.2/3 (2007): 140-161.

Steiner, George. *Real Presences*. Chicago: University of Chicago Press, 1991.

Sweeney, Eileen. "Literary Forms of Medieval Philosophy." *The Stanford Encyclopedia of Philosophy* (Summer 2013 Edition), edited by Edward N. Zalta. Accessed 30 November 2014. http://plato.stanford.edu/entries/medieval-literary/

A FEW REMARKS ON LOST POETS
Matthew Chelf

When we finally cross through the dusty, bloody desert and look back through the window, we see Cesare Tinajero

We see her, diminishing image, and slowly she is engulfed by yellowness and grayness, the dirt and the road, and consumed by an all-encompassing sky. She is gone, we continue hurling forward, the window—the window that frames it all—starts to pull apart and fade, and, before I realize it, it's just a window, the black frame of the car as we drive

We have to think about that window. The elusive window. The imperceptibly-now window. The lines, the immaterial frame that wisp away as you fix your eyes upon them

These lines linger invisibly, adding, framing, comprising The Work. These lines Cesarea abhorred, rejected, showed her contempt by holding them together

I want to hold these lines together, so I too can look through the window

§

Wind in my hair, I look out the window. Dust, haze, low bush, mountains. But something changes. I see the gleaming white bones of a carcass, magnificent, ringing hum. I consider Cesarea's silence

It's obvious. She wanted to become like gleaming white bones. Frequencies communing with silence

A myth will one day sweep across the desert, she will become the story of the stone who was interrupted from its torrid affair with nothingness

§

We imagine our passing along the highway as eviscerating a mirage. But there's no body to rip in a mirage. Just layers of deception and belief. The circle of the endless fuse that keeps burning

We want out of this motion, the release of the explosion

§

When I look back through the window the lines impose themselves like a viewfinder

The window dispenses a picture and then recedes

I hold Interpretation in my hand, an interpretation, dispensation, of a much larger, greater idea. (I am no Platonist but I must consider). The Symptom, perhaps, of impotence, the inability to hold the vista. The picture is the snap before the imminent detonation that marks the moment of reflection

I let the picture fly out the window and vanish, cannibalized by the air

§

The common fate of all mankind, Cesarea says, is the search for a place to live and a place to work

This is why I am here, this is why I have ever gone anywhere

This rule, this conviction—the damning truth—has left me searching sun bleached roads

We keep driving, but still we do not arrive outside the Work. I imagine it not like the solid white or black places you see in pictures. More like normal everyday things, just the window is held together

§

The slender beautiful woman of the dance hall— the stenographer for my general—the mother of visceral realism—finally, the elephantine woman of many lost poets left poetry for the sake of leaving

Living outside the Work, (a brown cracked field), singing in the sun in a wordless language deep. The lizards dance at her feet

<blockquote>
My barrier is the grave
It is why I sing
The grave is my heart
Diminutive and restive
Fill it with
Stones so I may be still
</blockquote>

Diminutive mass detour

Her barrier is the grave. The Work is the obstruction of virility

§

The driver of the car breaks speaks
Says a few things

The Work is many things

It might be the great life force, much like how we think of the Sun. But if you're burning in the desert then are you growing? The driver lifts hand to scorched earth

The Work might look like perfection but it's not. It's not Platonic. No ideal. Again, we act like lemmings throwing ourselves at this semblance of God.

Longing for the eternal timeless body. Yearning for transcendence and representation. But the Work is no Ideal

The Work is a potent metaphor for humanity's desire to merge with the universal and the eternal, to find representation and transcendence in the very stuff of artistic and cultural creation, and to find purpose in the utility of being reused and remade over and over, yes

Merger. Merger with the all. Merger with a meat grinder. We are something of a paste. A half-thing: a bleating paste: halfway between the chipper and the shooter. Moving moving. Between whole and dispersed. Forward. The churning. The Work is the churning

The driver continues onward

§

The driver has an afterthought

The Work is a framework of understanding as much as it is an artistic expression. It is a self-referential, closed system. Anything outside that sign system is inexplicable. Hence Cesarea, desert road you close your eyes against. Forward. The Churning

§

The Work includes excludes. Nothing new

§

We chased after "Sion" because we thought it would
lead us to Cesarea. We thought her soul resided
in the language. We loved her for her progeny:
language not words. Rude carving

We thought (I felt that) Cesara had seized that
windful caressing of the face and crystallized that
in the moment of poetry. How can someone have
such a delicate touch? To touch and handle time and
move with the rhythm. We chased Cesarea for her
touch

§

"Sion" is mirage (language mirage) for dynamite
blast underneath the fortification. The shattering
of ossified bone. Spray over the entire city. So we
chased Cesarea

§

Passenger back-seat driver-side in angry quandary:

Why did Cesarea need to lose herself in mirage?

Is "Sion" a message in a bottle left a sea, or is "Sion"
a landmine? The ignition—the hapless person

stumbling upon—is the definition in flux. Am I the beach walker on a lovely dusk evening who picks up an opaque brown glass bottle with a barnacled cork stopper? Am I the sweaty soldier who steps on the trigger? Do I discover or do I explode?

The moment of discovery—the surprise besmirching the face—the moment interrupting a peaceful ignition

To discover is to explode. Lost poets, wanderers, lead a life of constant casualty. We drive flaming into the desert heat when finally an airbag parachute catches us and cradles us into the gutter...

Democracy, Tragedy, Metonymy*
Kelly M.S. Swope

An earlier version of this essay, "Whitman, Ellison, Metonymy," was presented on March 7, 2015, at Lehigh University in Bethlehem, Pennsylvania, as part of a graduate student conference titled, "Literature and Social Justice."

I. The Two Poles of Tragedy

We are speaking today on literature and social justice. Perhaps this task would be less difficult for me were I sure that literature should serve social justice, or that a just world would produce fine literature, but I am not so sure of either. Of literature that purports to serve social justice causes, I seem to reserve a special skepticism, and I will not speak about the literature of a just world, since I do not believe that is where we live. On occasions like this, my thoughts turn to Friedrich von Schiller, the German poet who wrote in the wake of the French Revolution that the greatest work of art we can imagine would be the building up of a true political freedom for all humanity.[6] One has to examine that claim carefully. Schiller was not saying that great art will help us govern, or, as I thought when I first read him, that politics will make us better artists. He was

---

6   Friedrich Schiller, *Letters on the Aesthetic Education of Man*, Translated by Reginald Snell, Yale University Press, 1954, p. 25.

suggesting, rather, that an emancipated humanity would study the art of freedom, and, in time, make freedom its finest art. Believing this at the historical moment that he did must have put Schiller in a very disconsolate mood. Yet if all life is an animal farm, then I think of Schiller as having been most like the goat, singing with his fellow animals when they were joyful, and bleating with them when they had their throats cut. He wrote tragedies on the incompatibility of the noble passions with the frozen institutions of feudalism, though unlike, say, the tragedies of Shakespeare, Schiller's tragedies were more likely to culminate with the hero submitting himself, as in *The Robbers*, to be judged under the formal legal process, rather than under the jealous sword, for his main preoccupation, in lieu of metaphysical man, was political man, i.e., man who could conceive of liberty and equality concomitantly with the guillotine.

Bloody and inconclusive was the democratic revolution in Europe at the time of Schiller's death in 1805. His learned analogy, late in life, of democracy to the form of tragedy, was as historically as it was philosophically motivated. As Schiller saw it, man had successfully reasoned out the idea of equality in philosophy, yet in practice had proven tragically underprepared to realize it (hope for America was a generation away for many European democrats). It is interesting to compare the tragic liberalism of an early modern like Friedrich von Schiller, a German, to that of a later modern like Sir Isaiah Berlin, a Russo-English Jew who lived long enough to view the bloody upheavals of the Twentieth Century in hindsight. Berlin was not, as far as I know, an avid commentator on Schiller, but he did look to the flowering of Weimar Classicism for constant inspiration. In particular, Berlin was fond of J.G. von Herder's nascent value pluralism (often misidentified as cultural relativism), as well as one of Immanuel Kant's more poetic turns of phrase, in which the philosopher observed that out of the crooked timber of humanity, no straight thing was ever made.[7] Indeed, Herder's doctrine of "incommensurable objectivities" and Kant's one-liner contained the same positive observation; that man, at any given time, pursues so many uncommon ends that he cannot possibly make them all agree. Held up to the light of the Twentieth Century, which in Berlin's review reads like one sustained attempt to "straighten the timber," Herder and Kant's claims begin to ring with tragic sentiment. Berlin's late modernist revision of an older value pluralism was nothing if not a tragic philosophy developed out of witnessing humanity fall, not

---

7   Isaiah Berlin, *The Crooked Timber of Humanity*, Alfred A. Knopf, Inc., 1990, p. 70-90.

only from the high seat of Reason, but from the End of History itself. Every liberal in the West agreed that bringing Utopia down to Earth had brought catastrophic results. Only by returning to the Middle of History, where absolute values were volatile, refutable, and above all impermanent, was there any hope of making a fresh start in the postwar world order.

With the help of the first half of the Twentieth Century, therefore, Berlin improved Schiller's uncompleted tragic play into a cogent philosophical treatise. During the early modern round of revolution, Schiller understood democratic tragedy solely in terms of man's unworthiness before his new political ideal. Berlin, by the third or fourth round of blood and inconclusion, saw democratic tragedy as the permanent condition of free men, a struggle not of ultimate ideals, but of incommensurable values. Which absolutes are appealing, which appalling? That we even have to ask the question, again and again, is a tragedy in itself, for it suggests, first, that man is not improving morally with each passing generation, yet lives, at all times, in danger of regressing; second, it suggests that man does not have an earthly destiny, an End of History, waiting for him at the end of his struggle. Even so, for Berlin, it was better to have to sort through the good and the bad, mindful of vulgar, empirical humanity, than to take lives in the name of an absolute. "To demand more than [the opportunity to stand unflinchingly for the relative validity of one's convictions] is perhaps a deep and incurable metaphysical need," he writes at the end of "Two Concepts of Liberty"; "but to allow it to determine one's practice is a symptom of an equally deep, and more dangerous, moral and political immaturity."[8]

Let me return to the question of freedom with which I opened. How did an early-modern tragedian like Schiller view the experience of freedom compared to a late-modern liberal like Berlin? The difference between them can be explained with Berlin's own formula of "positive" versus "negative" liberty. Whereas Schiller fits with his contemporary, Kant, into the tradition of "positive" liberty as rational self-mastery, a tradition that, Berlin notes ironically, puts less emphasis on the the possibilities than on the limits of human self-knowledge (all that we cannot, and should not, try to master); Berlin, by contrast, was heir to the English liberalism of John Stuart Mill, a school that emphasized the negative, so-called "freedom from," pole of liberty. Now, my grouping of Schiller and Berlin into "positive" and "negative" poles is less for precision's sake than for the purpose of trying to discern what lies between

---

8   Isaiah Berlin, *Four Essays on Liberty*, Oxford University Press, 1969, p. 172.

them. For there seems to have been a shift, from the earlier to the later modern, in the orientation of the individual toward the institutions, the very citizens, of mass society. Schiller assumed that the experience of freedom obtained exclusively in the mutual cancellation of the "sensuous" and "rational" halves of the personality. "Positive" freedom was the individual's experience of setting himself free from the divergent dictates of nature and reason. Schiller's revised Kantianism held that the individual should design his personality in accordance with this idealized reconciliation of his divided subjectivity, disciplining his capricious nature, and relaxing his computational brain, on the way to becoming a more complete political self. Berlin had a historically altered set of concerns. His "negative" defense of liberty emerged from the shadows of European, and to an extent, East Asian, totalitarianism. His chief concern was that self-possessed individuals not be killed, one by one or en masse, by absolute authorities. For him, the peaceful coexistence of incommensurable values was preferable to the promotion of a single absolute. Individual freedom became about balancing self-mastery with social awareness. If I am to coexist even with my most estranged neighbors, it is my responsibility at least to tolerate them. I must therefore make some effort to "enter into" their world of values and judge the good and bad in them as best I can. More important than agreeing with my neighbor's values is recognizing them as legitimate *human* values that, insofar as they do not endanger the liberty of others, even though I may find them repugnant, are no less valid for repelling me. Note how the earlier modern, Schiller, was obsessed with perfecting human nature, while the later modern, Berlin, was obsessed with merely acknowledging it.

My question today is whether there were alternative forms of "tragic" democratic liberalism between these positive and negative poles represented by Schiller and Berlin. Were there, in the modern history of ideas, articulations of individual freedom that fell somewhere between rational self-mastery and negative tolerance, borrowing elements of each, while creating something distinct from them? There was such a tradition, I will argue, in the United States. Let me be clear in saying that I am not advocating for any kind of American exceptionalism, not in the least. If I intend anything, it is to provincialize Schiller and Berlin's views on liberty within their European context, and to do the same with the American writers I am about to discuss. My aim is not to show that these figures have nothing in common, but that, even while they played provincial roles in the world-historical drama, they shared all too much in the way of tragedy.

II. The American Art of Metonymy

Before I go on, I ask you to reflect on a Tragic American Century that unfolded between the early and late phases of modern Europe, a century wedged between Friedrich von Schiller and Isaiah Berlin which the former could not have anticipated, and the latter could absorb but impressionistically into his project. It would be unfair to say that they or similarly positioned European critics "missed" this phenomenon as they were fixed in contemplation of their home continent, but it is perfectly fair to say that the domestic battles of American democracy were a peripheral concern for them. The same provincialism of which I accuse European critics I also accuse the Americans I am about to discuss. But I think it worth commenting that, between the early modern period in Europe that anticipated fascist and communist totalitarianisms, and the late modern period that actualized them, a span of time over which European critics have obsessed for more than half a century, there was an entire century in the United States dedicated to the egalitarian inclusion, as well as the ruthless suppression, of racial minorities—notably the descendents of African American slaves, but others as well—within mainstream democracy. This pivotal century spanned from the 1860s, the decade of the Civil War and Emancipation, to the 1960s, the decade of Civil Rights and the Culture Wars. It was tragic in both of the senses I have already discussed: in Schiller's sense of proving inadequate to its own democratic ideal, in the institutions of Jim Crow, labor oppression, the Great Depression, and other ills; and in Berlin's sense of having to learn tolerance from the deadly consequences of intolerance, as seen from the culture of lynching to the segregation of the public schools. But it was also much more than these, and I am not going to pretend to summarize a hundred years in an essay as brief as this one. I have already reduced Schiller to a shadow of himself and called Isaiah Berlin a Weimar Classicist. Lest I do comparable damage to American history, let me step out of the historians' circle, in which I feel very uncomfortable, and enter the circle of literature, where I would like to speak about two artists who wrote eloquently from either pole of the Tragic American Century.

The two artists I am referring to are Walt Whitman and Ralph Ellison, writers who lived under historical circumstances so parallel that their lives, in retrospect, seem cosmically bound together. Ninety-five years separated their births; one hundred two years their deaths; ninety-seven years the publication of their seminal works; and ninety-nine years the most important political revolutions of their times. Both were stewards of the democratic ideal during a century that was largely antagonistic to it. Whitman was a pre-Emancipation writer who bloomed during the Civil War and waned during the Reconstruction. Ellison was a pre-Civil Rights writer who bloomed during the Sixties and waned during the Reagan Counterrevolution. Their writings merged in a single theme: the reconciliation of transcendental individuality with mass democracy. Whereas Whitman framed this reconciliation as the work of "recorders ages hence," Ralph Ellison turned to Whitman's generation for a precedent to uplift him.

A look at a few of their signature symbols will illustrate how I am framing these authors. Consider Whitman's poem, "The Dalliance of the Eagles," in which two eagles, representing two autonomous individualities, collide in mid-air as "Four beating wings, two beaks, a swirling mass tight grappling.../ the twain yet one, a moment's lull.../...then parting.../[in] separate diverse flight,/She hers, he his, pursuing."[9] The sudden amorous contact of the eagles suggests a transitory meeting of two personalities on divergent yet complementary trajectories. Now compare to Ellison's recurring figure of the jazz player, the utterly autonomous instrumentalist who seeks his freedom in the

---

9   Walt Whitman, *Leaves of Grass*, Rinehart & Co., 1972, p. 230.

fugitive harmonies of combination play, one moment conforming to the group objective, the next retreating into a chaos of improvisational narcissism. The jazz player moves on the same trajectory as the eagle, the individual colliding with the swirling mass, "the twain yet one," harmonizing, then parting; as if the important thing was not the idiosyncrasy of the individual, but her very substitutability; as if social roles were merely to be taken up at serendipitous moments, then abandoned in pursuit of other freedoms.

I have taken to calling this shared trope of Whitman and Ellison's metonymy, or the art of substituting names. The eagle and the jazz player are metonyms, names that invoke the reconciliation between transcendental individuality and democracy. Both Whitman and Ellison are conscious of the impermanence of such names. Whitman's eagles grapple for a mere "moment's lull" before breaking apart; Ellison's jazz player wheels forward for a spotlight solo only to hurry back into the darkness. By metonymy, then, I mean the symbolic naming of a form of freedom that cannot be experienced permanently.

Whitman writes, in the opening couplet of *Leaves of Grass*, "One's self I sing, a simple separate person;/Yet utter the word Democratic, the word En-Masse,"[10] as if he already knew of that ultimate reconciliation for which, later in the book, he will substitute a thousand different names—self, En-Masse, the leaves of grass, the eagles, the black slave, the map of America, and, not least, his own name. But what about these names? Does this inexhaustible chain of metonyms not suggest a fundamental discontinuity between the poet and his ideal? If there is one danger in Whitman's art of substitution, it is that no name holds valid over any other. For what signifies in his metonym is less the name itself than the purposiveness of its form. The purposive usage of the name invokes the democratic ideal without fully disclosing it. The paradox of Whitman's effusive naming is that he actually imposes incredible constraints upon himself. His verbal inexhaustibility is a function of his inability to disclose the final form of the reconciliation he imagines. The more I read him, the more I believe that his readers should be substituting questions wherever we find declarations on the page. Rephrased as a question, the opening couplet of *Leaves of Grass* might read, "How to sing my separate self while also speaking for you, the En-Masse?"

This is the question that in Whitman's prose writings

---

10   *Leaves of Grass*, p. 1.

gets worked out into the concept of "democratic personalism." It is the poet's most precise term for individual liberty:

> *To [personalism], all bends; and it is because toward such result democracy alone, on anything like Nature's scale, breaks up the limitless fallows of humankind, and plants the seed, and gives fair play, that its claims now precede the rest. The literature, songs, esthetics, &c., of a country are of importance principally because they furnish the materials and suggestions of personality for the women and men of that country, and enforce them in a thousand effective ways...Bibles may convey, and priests expound, but it is exclusively for the noiseless operation of one's isolated Self, to enter the pure ether of veneration, reach the divine levels, and commune with the unutterable.[11]*

To which Whitman attaches the footnote: "After the rest is satiated, all interest culminates in the field of persons, and never flags there." In other words, democracy serves the interest of personalism, "bends" to it as its inevitable best result. It is the political system that, by giving "fair (and equal) play" to all personalities, is singularly capable of actuating their full potential. Yet it is through the personality alone, "one's isolated Self," says Whitman, that it is

---

11 Walt Whitman, *Democratic Vistas*, Rinehart & Co., 1972, p. 516-17.

even possible to "commune with the unutterable." Here we run into a paradox. If political equality is the precondition for the flourishing of personalities, then the concept of personalism must have a healthy reciprocity with the concept of democracy. Democracy is necessarily the "unutterable" poetic ideal to which Whitman refers, for it is the very condition that must precede personalism in order to culminate in it.

Here we have the beginnings of a totalizing, if not a totalitarian, form of democracy. Libertarians would be uncomfortable with such unfettered reciprocity between subject and object. I sing my separate self while uttering the "En-Masse," the body politic, yet even as I utter its name, I am, in the same breath, unable to utter it, since it precedes me and conditions me totally. Personalism, therefore, is a free self-willing toward democracy that is also, somehow, compulsorily bound to it.

"How to sing my separate self while also speaking for you, the En-Masse?" Compare Whitman's question to the rhetorical question in the final line of Ralph Ellison's *Invisible Man*. The novel concerns a young black protagonist, expelled from a Southern HBCU, who then migrates north to New York City where he gets hired as a public orator for the Communist Party in Harlem. "Who knows," asks the Invisible Man at the end of his tale, "but that, on the lower frequencies, I speak for you?"[12] At first hearing, the question sounds much like Whitman's. Yet if there is a satisfactory answer, it depends on whether, in an apparently totalized world of racist manipulation, the protagonist can find his personal path to self-acceptance and freedom. Everyone he meets in the novel—rich white philanthropists, black college presidents, Communist Party officials—wants to use him for ulterior ends without regard for his individuality. No one "sees" him. The turning point in the novel comes when the protagonist, fleeing a riot in Harlem staged by the Communists, falls into a "hole in the ground" from which he begins to evaluate his social misery. In this subterranean schoolhouse of sorts, he studies the art of metonymy, formulating his personal struggle in terms of humanism and democracy more generally. He sees for the first time how his present miseries were caused by the undemocratic conditions that tormented him above ground, and he decides, there and then, to realign his life with an idealized concept of democracy in which his "humanity [would be] won by continuing to play in face of certain defeat."[13]

Unresolved at novel's end is what Ellison means by speaking for democracy "on the lower frequencies."

12   Ralph Ellison, *Invisible Man*, Vintage International, 1982, p. 581.

13   Ibid, p. 577.

He cannot only mean that individuals must improve their rational self-interest into an abstract "democratic personalism," as Whitman contends. It seems to me that the lower frequency must also encompass the struggle for self-actualization of a young black individual who does not conceive of himself, as others in the novel would have him, primarily in terms of his race, but in terms of his own humanity, a reading for which I find support in Ellison's critical writings on American literature. In the collection titled *Shadow and Act*, for example, Ellison argues that American modernists (i.e., white writers after Mark Twain), while doing much to advance the technical aspects of fiction writing, fundamentally evaded the calling of the American writer to confront the democratic ideal in literary form, specifically the question of where American Negroes fit into the national picture of democracy. Ellison believed that nineteenth-century writers such as Whitman, Melville, and Twain viewed the black slave as a symbol of America's unrealized democratic ideal, whereas writers after World War I—Hemingway, Fitzgerald, Steinbeck—failed to consider the unfinished emancipation of the Negro as a national moral crisis. It is not that these writers did not make black characters; they did. The problem for Ellison was that they did not lend humanity to these characters by examining racial questions on a deeper moral register, by which he means, "on the lower frequencies." According to Ellison, "The American writer has formed the habit of living and thinking in a culture that is opposed to the deep thought and feeling necessary to profound art; [hence his] precise and complex verbal constructions for converting goatsong into [a series of] carefully modulated squeaks."[14]

Goatsong, of course, is the etymology of the word tragedy. Recent social history was underwriting Ellison's tragic view of American literature. For him, the shortcomings of American literati reflected the social conditions out of which they arose. If the sin of segregation was institutionalized in national law and politics, then it could not but transfer to the products of high culture. The volatility of the Southern situation in particular influenced Ellison's decision to write *Invisible Man* alongside and against the American modernism of which he counted himself part. The crisis of his protagonist was the very crisis confronting Negro individuals after their Great Migration north from the Jim Crow South, a phenomenon that Ellison summarizes as follows:

> *In the South, the sensibilities of both blacks and whites are inhibited by the rigidly defined*

---

14   Ralph Ellison, *The Collected Essays of Ralph Ellison*, Random House, 1995, p.150

*environment. For the Negro there is relative
safety so long as individuality is suppressed...The
pre-individualistic black community discourages
individuality out of self-defense, [having] learned
through experience that the whole group is punished
[corporately] for the actions of a single member.[15]*

Without reducing Ellison's novel entirely to
historical allegory, the hero of *Invisible Man* might
be taken as a northbound black migrant whose search
for self-actualization is actually a search for the
form of individuality itself. But let me be absolutely
clear before I pursue this fragile point. In the above
passage, Ellison is not using "pre-individuality" as
an ontological category, but as a psychological and
political descriptor of the psychic damage inflicted
by historical racism in the United States. I cite the
term because it shows that for Ellison democratic
self-willing does not begin, as it does in Whitman,
with the fully self-actualized citizen, but with the
socialized person living out of sight and out of
earshot, prior to political individuality, "on the
lower frequencies." He continues:

*It is only when the individual, whether white or
black, rejects the pattern [of segregation] that he
awakens to the nightmare of his life...For it is
this unwillingness to resolve the conflict in keeping*

15 Ibid, p. 140.

> *with his democratic ideals [that has compelled
> him to force] the Negro down into the deeper
> levels of [his] consciousness, into the inner world,
> where reason and madness mingle with hope and
> memory and endlessly give birth to nightmare and
> to dream; down into the province of the psychiatrist
> and the artist, from whence spring the lunatic's
> fantasy and the work of art. It is a dangerous
> region even for the artist, and his tragedy lies in the
> fact that in order to tap the fluid fire of inspiration,
> he must perpetually descend and reencounter not
> only the ghosts of his former selves, but all of the
> unconquered anguish of his living.*[16]

I cannot find a better summary of the lesson of *Invisible Man* in all of Ellison's critical writings. The novel's Epilogue restates the above passage in a political vocabulary that emphasizes the democratic potential of the protagonist's life. Out of so-called "Negro pre-individuality," therefore, Ellison's hero discovers the form of self-actualizing individuality, and concludes his story, similarly to Whitman's essay, by anticipating the great democracy to come in America. Still, there is one crucial difference between Ellison's account of democratic idealism and his predecessor's. Recall that Whitman began *Leaves of Grass* with the fully self-actualized individual—"One's self I sing"—as the basis of his art of metonymy. His poetic reconciliation

---

16   Ellison, *Collected Essays*, p. 142

of transcendental individuality with mass democracy occurred by overwriting the conditions of his unemancipated reality with idealized egalitarian conditions. The world of Ellison's novel, by contrast, is one where socialized persons strive to achieve the form of individuality before any thought is given to "personalism." Consequently, Ellison's readers cannot presume as operative the same egalitarian conditions we find in *Leaves of Grass*. We must instead attune our ears to the lower frequencies.

In *Invisible Man*, the art of metonymy reconciles the pre-individuality of the Negro with the author's tragic vision of American democracy. However, attention should be given to how Ellison uses the word "Negro" as a metonym that extends beyond American blacks, describing all persons that battle against external determinations that obstruct the path to individual liberty. Note Ellison's generalizing tone in the following quote:

> *Being a Negro American involves a willed affirmation of self against all outside pressures—an identification with the group as extended through the individual self which rejects all possibilities of escape that do not involve a basic resuscitation of the original American ideals of social and political justice.*[17]

17 Ibid, p. 178.

To this Ellison attaches the coy afterthought, "And those white Negroes [could be] Negroes too—if they wish to be." There is a strain of both negative and positive liberty in this redefinition of the word "Negro"—the same reaching for total reconciliation of self and society that we saw in Whitman. Being Negro, for Ellison, means resisting oppressive determinations, regardless of color, while also willing one's self totally in the direction of the democratic ideals of social and political justice.

III. Tragic Democracy

Between rational self-mastery and value pluralism in modern Europe there was, demonstrably, an "American art of metonymy" that emphasized the reconciliation of transcendental individuality with mass democracy. Although this distinctively American articulation contained elements of positive self-making and negative pluralism, these depended absolutely on the individual's compulsive embrace of the democratic ideal. This was equally true for Walt Whitman as for Ralph Ellison, even though the former presupposed the integrity of the individual while the latter sought through art to achieve it. At opposite ends of the "Tragic American Century," then, I hear resolute calls for a totalized form of democracy.

This call was necessarily distinct from those of Friedrich Schiller and Sir Isaiah Berlin, European critics who watched the modern world-historical drama from a distant province. Just as their modern accounts of democratic liberalism looked past America's domestic struggles, so the Americans I discussed looked past tragic modernity in Europe. Like Berlin, I reject the relativization of the history of ideas, but I think it is important to recognize that the political ideals of these four moderns reflected local insights and local blindnesses. Yet, even as one considers them in their plurality, the least common denominator of their writings is the definitive association between liberal democracy and the literary form of tragedy. What can our conference on literature and social justice learn from this association? At the very least, we can learn something about building up a Twenty-First-Century Democratic Idealism out of the most resilient materials available to us.

BIBLIOGRAPHY

Berlin, Isaiah. *The Crooked Timber of Humanity*. Alfred A. Knopf, Inc., 1990.

Berlin, Isaiah. *Four Essays on Liberty*. Oxford University Press, 1969.

Ellison, Ralph. *Invisible Man*. Vintage International, 1982.

Ellison, Ralph. *The Collected Essays of Ralph Ellison*. Random House, 1995.

Schiller, Friedrich. *Letters on the Aesthetic Education of Man*. Translated by Reginald Snell, Yale University Press, 1954.

Whitman, Walt. *Democratic Vistas*. Rinehart & Co., 1972.

Whitman, Walt. *Leaves of Grass*. Rinehart & Co., 1972.

If you would like to write to any of the contributors, please first email theserpentclub@gmail.com and we will send you the appropriate mailing address. (And by "write" and "mailing address" we mean real letters on real paper, et cetera).

We also welcome submissions for forthcoming volumes.